Growing A Healthy
Community

This book has been provided by

**Carlisle Area Health and
Wellness Foundation**

to support improved health and wellness
in our communities.

Extreme
Athletes

Extreme Athletes

Other books in the History Makers series:

History MAKERS

Extreme Athletes

By Ron Horton

LUCENT BOOKS
An imprint of Thomson Gale, a part of The Thomson Corporation

THOMSON
—————✴—————™
GALE

Detroit • New York • San Francisco • San Diego • New Haven, Conn.
Waterville, Maine • London • Munich

14,194

LIBRARY OF CONGRESS CATALOGING-IN-PUBLICATION DATA

Horton, Ron (Ronald Everett)
    Extreme athletes / by Ron Horton.
        p. cm. — (History makers)
Includes bibliographical references and index.
    ISBN 1-59018-519-6 (hard cover : alk. paper)
    1. Athletes—Biography—Juvenile literature. 2. Extreme sports—Juvenile literature.
I. Title. II. Series.
    GV697.A1H67 2005
    796.04'6'0922—dc22
                                                    2004010559

Printed in the United States of America

Contents

FOREWORD

The literary form most often referred to as "multiple biography" was perfected in the first century A.D. by Plutarch, a perceptive and talented moralist and historian who hailed from the small town of Chaeronea in central Greece. His most famous work, *Parallel Lives*, consists of a long series of biographies of noteworthy ancient Greek and Roman statesmen and military leaders. Frequently, Plutarch compares a famous Greek to a famous Roman, pointing out similarities in personality and achievements. These expertly constructed and very readable tracts provided later historians and others, including playwrights like Shakespeare, with priceless information about prominent ancient personages and also inspired new generations of writers to tackle the multiple biography genre.

The Lucent History Makers series proudly carries on the venerable tradition handed down from Plutarch. Each volume in the series consists of a set of five to eight biographies of important and influential historical figures who were linked together by a common factor. In *Rulers of Ancient Rome*, for example, all the figures were generals, consuls, or emperors of either the Roman Republic or Empire; while the subjects of *Fighters Against American Slavery*, though they lived in different places and times, all shared the same goal, namely, the eradication of human servitude. Mindful that politicians and military leaders are not (and never have been) the only people who shape the course of history, the editors of the series have also included representatives from a wide range of endeavors, including scientists, artists, writers, philosophers, religious leaders, and sports figures.

Each book is intended to give a range of figures—some well known, others less known; some who made a great impact on history, others who made only a small impact. For instance, by making Columbus's initial voyage possible, Spain's Queen Isabella I, featured in *Women Leaders of Nations*, helped to open up the New World to exploration and exploitation by the European powers. Inarguably, therefore, she made a major contribution to a series of events that had momentous consequences for the entire world. By contrast, Catherine II, the eighteenth-century Russian queen, and Golda Meir, the modern Israeli prime minister, did not play roles of global impact; however, their policies and actions significantly influenced the historical development of both their own countries and their regional neighbors. Regardless of their relative importance in the greater historical scheme, all of the figures chronicled in the History Makers series made contributions to posterity; and their public achievements, as well as what is known about their private lives, are presented and evaluated in light of the most recent scholarship.

In addition, each volume in the series is documented and substantiated by a wide array of primary and secondary source quotations. The primary source quotes enliven the text by presenting eyewitness views of the times and culture in which each history maker lived, while the secondary source quotes, taken from the works of respected modern scholars, offer expert elaboration and/ or critical commentary. Each quote is footnoted, demonstrating to the reader exactly where biographers find their information. The footnotes also provide the reader with the means of conducting additional research. Finally, to further guide and illuminate readers, each volume in the series features photographs, two bibliographies, and a comprehensive index.

The History Makers series provides both students engaged in research and more casual readers with informative, enlightening, and entertaining overviews of individuals from a variety of circumstances, professions, and backgrounds. No doubt all of them, whether loved or hated, benevolent or cruel, constructive or destructive, will remain endlessly fascinating to each new generation seeking to identify the forces that shaped their world.

INTRODUCTION

The Nature of the Extreme Athlete

Extreme sports pit athletes against a variety of obstacles, some natural and some man-made. The athlete must go to extremes to overcome the obstacle, or execute a series of perilous moves in a certain amount of time on treacherous terrain. If the obstacle is properly negotiated and the moves are executed precisely, the outcome is awe-inspiring as the athletes smoothly manipulate the natural forces that surround them. But extreme sports are also highly dangerous, and if miscalculations occur, the outcome is catastrophic, ranging from certain bodily injury to the likelihood of death.

In light of stronger training regimens, better equipment, and more accessibility to a wide array of terrain, athletes are pushing the limits of human possibility further and further. No longer is the goal to simply complete the task safely and efficiently. An extreme athlete often pushes for speed, distance, or precision beyond what has been done before. At the dawn of the twenty-first century, most mountains have been climbed, most rivers have been paddled, and most waves have been surfed. It is the task of the extreme athlete to push these boundaries further, exploring new obstacles and greater dangers.

Extreme water sports include surfing, kayaking, wakeboarding, and windsurfing. Participants attempt to surf bigger waves, drop over larger waterfalls, or sail higher into the air off every swell. Oftentimes, the athlete perseveres and manipulates the craft successfully through one of nature's most powerful forces: water. Other times nature wins, churning the athlete-turned-victim beneath its tumultuous swirl.

Extreme sports can also be executed on land. These sports include rock climbing, BASE jumping, snowboarding, freeskiing, ice climbing, and motocross. Many extreme athletes on land attempt to negotiate a set course, which may be either man-made or of natural origin. The climber attempts a section of unexplored rock or ice, trying to either make a first ascent or beat a previous climber's time. The freeskier dodges in and out of trees at breakneck speeds,

10

avoiding rocks and limbs along the way, on steep slopes with avalanche potential. Often these land sports take the athlete high into the air. BASE jumpers launch off of cliffs or structures more than a mile high with only a parachute attached. Controlled free-fallers jump over a thousand feet with simply a rope and harness for protection. Motocross riders speed their bikes over huge jumps, performing backflips on their heavy machines. Even climbers defy gravity when they choose to leave their ropes behind and take the ultimate challenge of soloing a route without the aid of any gear.

A champion BASE jumper leaps from one of the world's tallest towers. BASE jumpers experience a few seconds of free fall before deploying a parachute.

Reasons for Extreme Sports

Extreme sports come in all sorts of interesting forms, and extreme athletes come in all shapes and sizes. Men, women, adults, and children pit their bodies and wills against an abundance of obstacles to perform amazing feats. As humans continue to push themselves further and further against the elements, extreme sports will continue to push the borders of attainability. Author Brendan Koerner describes this phenomenon in "Extreeme":

> Extreme sports not only satisfy the need for excitement in an increasingly boring world. They also provide an outlet for the kind of creativity and individual expression often squashed in a homogenized culture of chain stores and mini malls. While baseball and football remain virtually unchanged from generation to generation, extreme athletes are constantly fiddling with the formulas to create new disciplines. [1]

Extreme skier Kristen Ulmer provides a vivid example of the difference between extreme sports and conventional sports: "It's one thing to be a really good basketball player, but imagine if every time you missed a basket, somebody would shoot you in the head. It would be a lot more exciting, right?" [2] Ulmer's anecdote describes the type of action contemporary society has grown accustomed to; people are looking for excitement, and they want it right away.

In recent years, extreme sports have reached a wider audience through the media, advertisements, and popular culture. Author Maryann Karinch explains how these athletes affect society:

> Extreme athletes are heroes because they try something harder, faster, longer. Anyone can benefit from their insights and relate to them as people. Their goal is not a score or a medal. . . . The prize they want is the full-bodied thrill of accomplishment and the lessons they offer you are how to achieve it. [3]

While more people are becoming familiar with and choosing to participate in extreme sports, certain athletes stand out for their dedication, skill, and performance at extreme endeavors. Laird Hamilton revolutionized what size waves a surfer could navigate on a board. Dan Osman pushed the limits of controlled free-falling on climbing ropes. Freeskier Kristen Ulmer successfully completed many first descents, including the first female descent of the Grand Teton in Wyoming. Kayaker Tao Berman holds world records for height, distance, and speed/altitude descents in a kayak. Glenn Singleman BASE

Motorcyclist Mike Metzger soars through the air while performing a fully extended rock solid at a freestyle competition.

jumped the world's highest cliff the same year he learned the sport. Mike Metzger successfully completed the first backflip on a full-size motorcycle, repeating the trick with no feet on his bike just months later. These six extreme athletes embody the courage and determination that it takes to push the limits of their respective sports, becoming truly noteworthy individuals in the process.

CHAPTER 1

Laird Hamilton: The Art of Tow-In Surfing

Laird Hamilton is considered by some to be one of the greatest athletes of the last century. Adept at surfing, sailboarding, long-distance paddling, and tow-in surfing, he is an all-around waterman. Growing up a stone's throw away from some of the world's greatest surf breaks, he has spent his whole life swimming and surfing big waves. His knowledge of the ocean and ability to manipulate his body and navigate his board through all types of conditions makes him one of the strongest, most versatile surfers in the world. With more than thirty years of experience behind him, nearly a third of which were spent towing in to bigger and bigger waves behind a jet ski, Hamilton amazes spectators by surfing the world's largest waves.

Early Life in Paradise

Laird Hamilton was born Laird John Zerfas in northern California on March 2, 1964. His parents, L.G. Zerfas and JoAnn Zyirek, were surfers who met in high school. Laird was born at the University of California medical center in San Francisco through an experimental birthing procedure. JoAnn gave birth to Laird in a bathysphere, which allowed him to float more freely with less pressure during the last five hours of labor. The experimental results for such procedures varied, but all of the children were above normal weights and heights for newborns.

Shortly after Laird's birth, L.G. joined the merchant marine. However, he never returned home and so JoAnn dated several other local surfers. Eventually she moved to the North Shore of the island of Hawaii with one of her boyfriends. It was there in 1967 that young Laird chose Billy Hamilton to be his father. Billy, a world-famous surfer and board designer, describes the experience: "As I look back now, I realize it was my destiny. . . . I hadn't even met his mom yet. I was bodysurfing . . . and I saw this little blonde-haired kid rolling around in the shore break. I came up to him, and there was an immediate connection. We're bodysurfing around, he's got his arms wrapped around my neck, we just locked into each other." [4] After bodysurfing that day, Laird told Billy that he wanted him to be his father.

Becoming Laird Hamilton

Billy and JoAnn met later that day, and were immediately attracted to one another. JoAnn chose Billy over her current boyfriend, and a courtship ensued. They were married a few months later. Laird followed his new father around everywhere, curious as to the man's

All-around waterman Laird Hamilton is considered one of the greatest athletes of the last one hundred years.

every move. On Oahu, he soon learned how to surf the coastal waters, first riding tandem with his father steering the board and later, at the age of three, on his own custom-designed Hamilton board. This early initiation to surfing at some of Hawaii's greatest beach breaks gave Laird the experience and confidence necessary to become a great, well-rounded surfer.

Seeking to avoid the ever-growing tourist crowds of Oahu's North Shore, the Hamiltons soon moved to Kauai's Wainiha Valley, a more isolated region even closer to some of Hawaii's best surf breaks. Billy continued to design surfboards, and the rest of the Hamilton family enjoyed uncrowded beaches and endless waves. Paradise did not come without struggle, however. JoAnn recalls that young Laird was quite a handful, ripping the tops off of sunbathing women and even punching a teacher in the stomach when she told him not to cut in line.

Suffering Prejudice

While Laird caused plenty of trouble, he also suffered a great deal at the hands of his peers. As the only white student in his remote village's small school, he learned some hard lessons. In California, the blond-haired, blue-eyed child would have blended into the crowd, but in Wainiha, he was an outsider. Throughout his early years in school, Laird suffered daily beatings from his peers simply because he looked and acted differently. This experience taught him the importance of self-defense and personal strength at an early age.

Much of Laird's personal strength came from his love of the outdoors and the confidence that those experiences provided him. When he was not hiking and surfing with his father, he would hunt wild pigs or work in the fields near his house. Billy Hamilton recalls taking his eight-year-old son to a sixty-foot cliff above Waimea Falls. Laird took one look at the lagoon below, looked back at his father, and then jumped off the edge, landing in the water below. From that moment on, Billy realized that his son did not possess the normal childhood fear of gravity or water. He later stated, "He's been bold since day one and hell bent on living life to the extreme." [5]

Laird continued to hone his skills by taking part in the amazing surfing opportunities that surrounded his home. By the age of ten, he was surfing waves ten feet high—and higher—with his father. Laird describes what it was like learning to surf under the supervision of a true master: "My whole upbringing, I wanted to ride waves the way my dad could."[6] Laird continued to follow in his father's footsteps, always eager to push his skills on bigger waves. Learning to maneuver his board through ten-foot waves at such a young age provided a great initiation, and these experiences made the transition to big-wave surfing, surfing waves of fifteen feet and higher, much easier for him.

Hamilton rides a massive wave during the filming of a feature movie. Hamilton's intense training regimen allows him the confidence to surf the world's largest waves.

Choosing the Surf over School

At school, Laird continued to suffer racist slurs and frequent beatings at the hands of his classmates. He convinced his parents to let him drop out of Kauai's Kapaa High School at the age of sixteen so that he could work and surf more. Laird explains his decision:

> Being a minority, you're forced to become a man. You're forced to become strong and courageous, [to] develop the spiritual. . . . That's part of the reason why the ocean means so much to me. Because that's the one place I could find true equality. The wave comes, and it lands on you, me, and the next guy. It's bigger than human relations. . . . I gravitated towards it. I wanted to be out there more than on land. The ocean was the only place I wanted to be.[7]

After dropping out of school, Laird found work on a local construction crew. But he was soon discovered by an Italian fashion magazine shooting on location in Kauai. Due to his muscular physique, he was asked to participate in the shoot. After the photo shoot ended, he received an offer to pose for a GQ shoot on Oahu, where he met fashion photographer Bruce Weber, who introduced him to the world of fashion art. Intrigued by the fashion industry, Laird Hamilton moved to Los Angeles, California, in the early 1980s.

In Los Angeles, Hamilton modeled for several magazines. He also modeled for the surfwear company Sunbreaker, receiving monthly payments for wearing their clothing in advertisements. Poor management led to the company's bankruptcy, however, and Hamilton found himself, with the exception of a few modeling jobs, unemployed in an unfamiliar, inhospitable city. The crowded surfing conditions and lack of outdoor activities left Hamilton questioning his choice to live in Los Angeles. He says about that time, "Cities are lonely places . . . I felt my gills drying up. My whole youth was being wasted."[8]

A New Board Sport

To combat his loneliness, Hamilton began boardsailing (also known as windsurfing), a water sport that uses an oversized surfboard and a sail to harness wind like a sailboat. He explored the local reservoirs in search of gusty winds and high speed. Hamilton quickly grew homesick, however. In 1986 he returned to Hawaii and settled on Maui, where he joined a group of radical boardsailors who were pushing the limits of the sport. Rather than riding normal-size waves close to shore, these athletes were sailing farther offshore and riding over-twenty-foot waves, launching their boards high in the air and landing with precision in choppy surf.

Shortly thereafter, at the age of twenty-two, Hamilton entered a speed-boardsailing competition in Port-Saint-Louis, France, and defeated the French champion, Pascal Maka. In the process he broke the European speed record of thirty-six knots. As if these honors were not enough, Hamilton returned to Hawaii with a two-year sponsorship from the sailboard company Neil Pryde. This contract paid him more than three thousand dollars a month to boardsail and model for ads.

During this time period, Hamilton continued to surf big waves on his surfboard and push the limits of speed on his sailboard. While many of his fellow surfers and boardsailors filled their schedules with competitions and judged performances, Hamilton devoted his time to performing a variety of paddling stunts that gained international attention. Lying chest down in the paddle position on a long, lightweight surfboard, Hamilton hand-paddled twenty-six miles from Molokai to Oahu through strong currents and huge gusts of wind. And, in 1990, in top shape from countless daily hours of surfing and boardsailing, Hamilton and fellow waterman Buzzy Kerbox were the first people to paddle surfboards the entire nineteen miles across the English Channel.

First Steps Toward Tow-In Surfing

Dabbling in a variety of different water sports led Hamilton to his first attempt at combining boardsailing with big-wave surfing. The standard big-wave surfer balances on the board without any attachments. Hamilton believed that the use of straps on his board to lock in his feet would provide him with the extra balance necessary to perform a variety of tricks that no other surfer could execute on a standard surfboard, such as aerial 360s and daring cutbacks on large waves. These minor additions to his board sparked criticism from many traditional surfers who felt that changing the sport in any way was wrong. Ignoring his critics, Hamilton continued to develop his ideas for evolving the sport of surfing to include mastering bigger waves, performing more daring maneuvers, and harnessing longer rides.

In his pursuit of the biggest wave, Hamilton looked to Hawaii's past. Folk tales described natives paddling canoes into big waves, jumping onto wooden planks, and riding into shore. Hamilton dreamt of going beyond these early methods to ride waves in the "unridden realm," a term coined by late big-wave surfer Mark Foo to describe immense waves offshore that no surfer could paddle into. This era in the early nineties marked the dawn of the "tow-in surfing" revolution.

Pushing the Boundaries

In 1992 Laird Hamilton teamed up with fellow surfers Derrick Doerner and Buzzy Kerbox to tow in to the twelve- to fifteen-foot waves of the Backyards, a surf break just off Oahu's North Shore. Tow-in surfing had been experimented with in the 1930s using speedboats and helicopters, but the idea was never fully explored due to lack of interest and limited resources. As a result, many amazing surf breaks just offshore had remained unridden.

Using an inflatable Zodiac boat, the surfers charged through the waves some hundred yards beyond the surf break. Hamilton jumped out of the boat and onto his traditional big-wave board, grabbing the towrope attached to the boat. The boat sped up as Hamilton held the rope and crouched down low on his board. Just as the fifteen-foot wave broke, he dropped the towrope and glided across its crystal blue crest, angling sharply and dropping into the wave. His ride, unattainable without the aid of the boat and towrope, lasted a

Hamilton (holding board at far left) poses with a crew of the world's best tow-in surfers and their specially designed towboards.

remarkable forty-five seconds. Less than a minute of surfing forever changed the possibilities of the sport in the minds of these three tow-in pioneers, and raised the question, "what next?"

In February 1993, Kerbox, Doerner, and Hamilton teamed up again to tackle twenty-foot waves off the coast of Maui. The tow-in surfers succeeded in catching ten to fifteen waves per hour, three times the amount a standard paddling surfer catches. Hamilton credits both his colleagues and himself for their vision: "We all felt that big waves could be ridden better than they've been ridden. . . . We dreamed about it. Then we figured out a way to do it."[9]

Evolving Tow-In Practices

Later that same year, Hamilton and Kerbox began exploring other surf breaks off Maui. One of their test spots was a legendary outer reef break near Piahe Valley. Offshore from this valley lies the surf break known as Jaws. Writer Joel Achenbach describes the surf break:

> Jaws is the creation of a peculiar reef . . . allowing surfers to ride waves as intimidating as tsunamis. Estimates vary, but a small wave at Jaws has a 20-foot face, and surfers . . . talk about waves with barrels so huge you could park a Winnebago in them. They talk about the violence of a wave's lip as it crashes into the impact zone. . . . They respect Jaws.[10]

Jaws was rumored to have waves larger than thirty-five feet in size. Waves that size had never before been ridden on a surfboard. Several people, including Hamilton, had navigated these waves before on a sailboard, but no one had ever surfed Jaws. Though the waves were not at their peak height due to weather conditions during Hamilton's inaugural ride, he did manage to ride several waves higher than twenty feet.

In preparation for riding these enormous waves, Hamilton's tow-in crew replaced the Zodiac boat with a faster, more powerful jet ski. This change increased towing speed and was safer in the event a rescue was necessary. In 1993 Hamilton had also designed a board whose shape and strength could handle the speed and force of immense waves, one that was used only for riding waves, not paddling into them. The seven-foot-ten-inch-long and sixteen-inch-wide board had foot straps bolted on the top to prevent slipping and to allow for aerial maneuvers and choppy turns at high speed. With these changes, Hamilton and the others would be able to tackle these bigger waves in the unridden realm.

Hamilton's Popularity Soars

The year 1994 saw a boost in popularity for Hamilton, as well as for tow-in surfing. He was becoming the best big-wave surfer, with a reputation for going bigger, faster, and further than any of his contemporaries. Hamilton was featured in twenty-seven of the twenty-eight shots for *Surfing* magazine's article titled "Power Surfing." He also appeared as the only tow-in surfer referred to by name in Bruce Brown's surf movie *The Endless Summer II*. Matt Warshaw's book *Mavericks* describes one of Hamilton's twenty-foot rides at Jaws for the film:

> He's strapped to a yellow and red toothpick of a surfboard, feet spread wide, thighs and knees slightly turned out, and as the wave gobbles and spits just a few yards behind him, he cuts a flaring sideways S across the face, and does it again—fusing big-wave riding and high performance surfing like he was buttering toast—then launches off the crest of the now spent swell, arcs through the air, and softly touches down in the flat water. [11]

Despite all of this focused attention on Hamilton as the main tow-in surfer, he was still regularly praised by his fellow surfers for his ability and style. Derrick Doerner comments, "He's an animal. Me and Buzzy are riding waves; Laird just casually plays with them." [12] Throughout the early evolution of tow-in surfing, Hamilton showed the most precision and skill when riding the biggest waves. He would routinely step up to larger obstacles, refusing to shy away from danger, exhibiting his extreme confidence and mastery of big-wave surfing.

Marriage and Fatherhood

During 1994 Hamilton married a Brazilian-born clothing designer named Maria whom he had met while bodysurfing at Waimea Bay. Maria had been a top competitive gymnast for nearly a decade in her native country, but had grown tired of the strict regulations within the sport. The two shared much in common with their disdain for standard competition and a love of adrenaline-charged

Hamilton carves a critical cutback turn during a tow-in session at Jaws. By the mid-1990s Hamilton was already recognized as the top tow-in surfer on the planet.

water sports. The couple had a daughter, Izabela, in 1995. Much like Hamilton's own childhood, Izabela grew up amid the sun and surf of Hawaii.

The family lived on the island of Maui while Hamilton perfected his tow-in skills. An accomplished bodyboarder in her own right, Maria attempted tow-in surfing big waves on Hamilton's board once, but almost lost her life when she fell from the board into the churning mass of white water. Sheer will, physical strength, and the desire to not leave her daughter motherless enabled her to survive a long time underwater.

Waiting for the Perfect Wave

Surfing depends on tides, storms, swells, and the general mood of the ocean to create waves, and sometimes there are no waves to surf. Hamilton focused much of his time during the mid-1990s experimenting with new board designs, developing tow and rescue techniques, and practicing his craft on larger and larger waves. Even though Hawaii is considered to have some of the greatest surfing on the planet, it had not seen a big-wave season since the late 1960s. With the ability to tow in to some of the biggest waves ever surfed, Hamilton waited for the ocean to comply and provide the proper surf conditions.

Another major focus for Hamilton during this time was hosting a TV show called *The Extremists*. Each episode of the two-season-long program took Hamilton to a new spot around the globe to partici-pate in extreme sports such as bungee jumping, rock climbing, and kite surfing, among others. All the time and energy spent focusing on his career eventually led to the breakdown of his marriage to Maria. The two divorced in 1997, but maintain close ties and share joint custody of their daughter.

In early 1997, during the same time period as his divorce from Maria, Hamilton met volleyball cham-pion Gabrielle Reece, who was vacationing in Hawaii. The two connected immediately as incredible athletes at the top echelons of their respective sports. After a brief courtship, Hamilton and Reece were married on November 30, 1997. Unlike his previous marriage, both Hamilton and his wife were equally busy focus-ing on their own careers, so they enjoyed their time together while understanding the necessity of their times apart.

tim-mckenna.com

Shortly after marrying Reece, Hamilton's years of patiently waiting for big waves paid off. Meteorologists began predicting huge storms and swells for the North Pacific so Hamilton made plans to be there when the storm hit. On January 28, 1998, Hamilton got the chance to test his skills against the biggest waves he had ever attempted to surf: waves reaching thirty feet and high-er. Buzzy Kerbox comments on the experience: "Jaws was very, very heavy that Wednesday. . . . Although the swell direction wasn't perfect, it was the biggest day rid-den out there. Laird Hamilton, Dave Kalama, and I all rode huge waves that raised the bar for big waves at Jaws forever."[13] This experience at Jaws set new standards in big-wave surfing and left Hamilton and the other surfers wanting more.

The Ride of a Lifetime

Hamilton found what he was looking for, and the biggest ride of his life came on August 17, 2000, in Teahupoo, Tahiti. Wave forecasters watching the storm patterns of the Pacific Ocean predicted big surf in this area, and Hamilton made certain that he would be there when the weather hit. He had ridden waves of similar heights at Jaws, but none with the sheer force, magnitude, or thickness that were breaking that day. The curl of the wave's tube literally closed out and

Hamilton charges through a deadly barrel at Teahupoo during the biggest ride of his life, in August 2000.

exploded, and a surfer trapped in its clutches would do the same. Wave forecaster Mike Perry describes Teahupoo:

> Imagine this: Stretch your arm out away from your body and bend it at the elbow. Picture your entire bent arm as an azure-blue, vertical cliff of warm, clear, Tahitian water. . . . Get stuck in there, and Teahupoo will do to a surfer what a meat tenderizer does to a clove of garlic. [14]

That day Hamilton was towed out into the dangerous surf. At the moment Hamilton released the towrope, the wave was in full bloom, thick and long. He sped down the face, carved back into its fullness, and danced within the curl that was forming over his head. He charged full speed down the center of the wave as it began to surround him, fully covering his body. As a massive crash of white water exploded just above the shallow reef, Hamilton narrowly exited the maelstrom unscathed. Billy Hamilton describes the scene: "With that wave in Tahiti . . . clearly the line has been drawn in the sand, and there is only one set of footprints on the other side. I think it is important for people to understand that when they see him riding the waves that he rides, if he falls, he will die. . . . He would have been vaporized on the reef if he had fallen on that wave." [15]

The Aftermath of Teahupoo

If the world was not convinced that Laird Hamilton rode the biggest waves on earth, that August in Tahiti provided irrefutable evidence. Hamilton's own words on the experience are simple: "If you see waves like what you saw here and you don't believe that there's something greater than we are, then you've got some serious analyzing to do and you should go sit underneath a big tree for a long period of time." [16] The film footage from that day, combined with Jaws footage and family videos, was edited to create a short documentary titled *Laird*. Later that same year, Hamilton was asked to perform his surfing skills at Jaws for the big screen as a stunt double for the James Bond film *Die Another Day*.

When he is not traveling the globe surfing the world's biggest waves or on location for various films, Hamilton lives on Kauai with his wife, Gabrielle, who gave birth to their first child, daughter Reece, in October 2003. Named the Surf Industry Manufacturers Association's Waterman of the Year for 2003, Hamilton still pushes the limits of big-wave riding, setting his sights on larger waves and greater feats. He says of his future, "I want to go after the world speed sailing record. I want to

With his cutting-edge waveriding invention, the hydrofoil board, Hamilton achieves greater speeds with less drag than on a conventional surfboard.

ride bigger waves. I want to try and invent some new sports, combine some existing ones. I want to be creative." [17]

Hamilton has already begun using his creativity to develop a new type of surfboard known as the hydrofoil board. On this new invention, the board's rider is attached to the deck using boots and bindings. A metal strut is bolted to the bottom of the fiberglass board and leads to an aluminum hydrofoil, usually four feet beneath the board. The hydrofoil elevates the surfer and board just above the water while planing underneath the surface, thus decreasing surface tension and allowing for greater speeds. Hydrofoil boards will ultimately enable their riders to glide along the biggest swells the ocean can create.

Hamilton remains the most recognized tow-in surfer. He excels at all aspects of surfing and is considered an all-around waterman, holding multiple world records in a variety of water sports. His performances at both Jaws and Teahupoo will forever remain a testament to Hamilton's accomplishments in the evolution and perfection of tow-in surfing on the world's biggest waves.

CHAPTER 2

Dan Osman: Pushing Gravity's Limits

In 1991 rock climber Dan Osman amazed the rock-climbing community with his ropeless ascent of both a physically and mentally demanding route called Gun Club in West Virginia's New River Gorge. The soft-spoken Asian American climber repeatedly showed the world his determination and skill by climbing extremely difficult routes, often without the safety of a rope, ultimately creating a new sport that pushes the limits of both climbing gear and human ability. Though he had many supporters, Osman also managed to acquire a wide range of critics during his short life, including traditional climbers, park rangers, and law officers.

Dan Osman's life was a paradox in many ways. Although he timed most climbs and hikes in an attempt to beat previous records, he was notoriously late almost everywhere he went. Though he was an accomplished carpenter, his own house remained a cluttered mess with projects left half-finished or never started. And even though he had a strict upbringing, raised in the samurai ethic by his Japanese-American father, he often tested authority in the form of unpaid tickets and driving without a license. Anomalies of character aside, Dan Osman was a passionate, creative, and talented climber, and his death, though not a shock, remains a tragic occurrence that affected the numerous friends and fans he acquired during his brief life.

Instilling the Bushido Ethic

Daniel Eugene Osman was born in 1963 in Corona, California. His mother, Sharon Louise Burks, was a horse trainer and two-time world champion barrel racer. His father, Les Osman, worked as a police officer, assigned to the tactical SWAT team. Dan also had a sister, Andrea, whom he was close to his entire life.

Dan was raised in the samurai's Bushido ethic. Bushido, meaning "the way of the warrior," involves strict discipline both mentally and physically. Young Daniel studied aikido and kung fu, just as his father and grandfather before him had. This background in martial

29

Dan Osman constantly challenged the accepted limits in the sport of rock climbing until his tragic death in 1998.

arts led to his respect for others, his understanding of tradition, and his strong belief in loyalty and honor. Dan's great-grandfather was a direct descendant of the Takeuchis, a samurai family from Japan. He immigrated to Hawaii in the 1890s, and was killed protecting the landowner for whom he worked during an uprising on a sugar plantation. Dan Osman not only inherited his forefather's bloodline, he also inherited a stubborn tenacity in standing up for his own beliefs, another Bushido trait.

During Dan's youth, Les Osman encouraged his son to push his physical limits within the realms of his chosen sports: martial arts and track and field. His mother also encouraged him to explore new paths, and through her urgings, he tried rock climbing at the age of twelve. By today's standards, Dan was not a natural, but his training in martial arts and his attention to discipline led him to continually succeed in both team sports and rock climbing.

In his late teens, Dan excelled at pushing his limits, both by small increments and by leaps and bounds. He participated in track throughout his high school years as a high jumper. This early athletic interest taught him how to measure his success incrementally. He could beat an opponent by mere inches, hurling his muscled torso over the high bars with innate dexterity.

His other passion, BMX bicycling, allowed Dan to defy gravity—in the half-pipe and using a variety of natural obstacles. He not only rode at local skate and bike parks but spent much of his time exploring the trails surrounding Corona. Throughout this time period, Dan continued to rock climb, and it became his favorite pastime.

The Climbing Lifestyle

Shortly after graduating from high school in Corona in 1981, Dan Osman went to Yosemite to explore the park's abundance of climbing opportunities. In Yosemite he lived minimally, sleeping in a tent and working as often as was necessary to buy food and gear for his next climb. This hand-to-mouth lifestyle would stick with him throughout his life. During this time, he climbed on a daily basis, gaining both strength and experience as a climber.

During his stay in Yosemite, Osman climbed many of the classic routes in the area and worked on developing new climbing routes in the park. Local climber John Bachar, who was known for his ability to free solo, or climb difficult routes without ropes, was an early influence on Osman. Osman respected Bachar for both his mental and physical strength, stating his feelings simply: "John embodied my vision of what free climbing should be. . . . I admired his boldness

Osman airs above the lip of a half-pipe on his BMX bicycle. Osman's passion for bike riding allowed him to defy gravity in ways besides climbing.

and purity."[18] At Yosemite, Osman climbed with ropes, but he also began free soloing. Some of Osman's early notoriety came from his ability to climb long, hard routes without any ropes.

In 1982, Osman and his friend Tom Gilje set out to climb a difficult route called Insomnia Crack without ropes. This climb had been done without the use of protective gear only once, by John Long, a famous local climber. When the pair began climbing unroped, the rock wall was in full range of the sun and quite hot, which made the holds slippery. Gilje, an accomplished climber, backed off the route and returned to the ground. Most climbers would have made the same decision as Gilje, but Osman did not. He continued to climb the sunbaked route to its summit. This determination to complete goals he set for himself, even in the face of great danger, was one of Osman's signature traits.

Finding a Home

After several years of perfecting his rock-climbing skills and honing his solo abilities, Osman moved to Lake Tahoe, California, where he continued to climb. He free soloed a Lake Tahoe area classic climb named Space Walk. Although the route involved incredibly technical, thin-crack climbing skills on a slightly overhanging angle, Osman climbed it without a rope the first time he ever attempted it.

During this time, Osman also married Katherine Noyes and fathered a daughter, Emma, born in 1989. The relationship between Osman and Noyes was brief, and he blamed the breakup, in part, on his focus on his climbing career. Even though Emma remained in the custody of her mother, living in Gardnerville, Nevada, Osman maintained close ties with his daughter.

In Tahoe, Osman began creating new climbing routes on cliffs at a sacred Washoe Indian site known as Cave Rock. Although the spot had become overrun with tourists and trash, Osman picked it as a project to clean up and establish as a new climbing area. He began creating very challenging rock climbs around the cave over the course of the late 1980s and early 1990s. Some of these climbs were categorized at the hardest level for that time period, and Osman created them using ropes and climbing gear to protect himself from falling during the incredibly difficult moves.

Exploring the Roots of Fear

In 1989 Osman began pushing his limits climbing on ropes at Cave Rock. While establishing his hardest route there, Phantom Lord, he kept falling at the most difficult spot. Even though his rope kept him from hitting the ground, falling into midair was still dangerous and frightening. This experience gave Osman insight into his future as a rock climber. He discovered that what held him back from climbing to his full ability was his fear of falling.

Osman began purposefully taking falls on his climbing rope in order to embrace his fear and fully push his climbing potential. Even after the route was established, Osman would often climb high above the last point where the rope was attached to the rock and drop in a free-fall fashion until the rope grew taut, stopping him above the ground. By confronting his fears, Osman grew stronger as a climber. However, he yearned to push these limits even further.

Osman's 1991 free solo of the route Gun Club, in West Virginia's New River Gorge, gave him instant notoriety. Clad in striped climbing tights, ominously adorned with skulls and crossbones, Osman successfully climbed the incredibly difficult route unroped for videographer Jay Smith. Smith describes the moment:

> His climbing was solid and relaxed as if he was an inch off the ground. He floated up the holds in perfect rhythm. Taking his time, never stopping. . . . Where . . . before he had fallen, he now floated. . . . Through my lens I watched one of the world's best climbers dance up the face [of the rock]. [19]

Osman's free-solo ascents were the talk of the climbing community, but he still had to support himself through means other than climbing. An accomplished carpenter, Osman worked a variety of construction jobs around the Tahoe and Reno area. Although he did receive some endorsements from various companies that used his image to sell their products, he often had to track down advertisers in order to receive payment for his services. Even with this lack of payment, Osman continued to climb incredibly hard routes and fall longer distances on ropes.

Osman's desire to fully explore his fears led him to begin questioning how far he could fall on a rope. He devised a fall from Yosemite's Rostrum Wall. He used standard protective climbing gear—a rope attached to the cliff through metal wedges, nylon slings, and oval-shaped metal carabiners—but he made knife cuts in the nylon slings so that they would break as he fell. Below the gear that was set up to fail, he attached gear to catch his fall two hundred feet above the ground. He describes the incident: "Even though I knew I'd set up the gear to fail, my instinct as a climber was that it should hold. So with each pop I let out a small scream. The acceleration was so incredible; when I finally stopped moving all I felt was a great relief and exhilaration at having pulled it off." [20] Osman took every climber's greatest concern, falling on gear that does not hold, and exploited it to gain insight into the notion of fear itself.

Exploring Bigger Falls

In the early 1990s, Dan Osman's athletic emphasis shifted from climbing to falling. Throughout his career as a controlled free-faller, Osman

Osman scales the Gun Club route in West Virginia without the aid of ropes during his famous free-solo ascent in 1991.

used only climbing ropes and climbing equipment to protect him in his falls. As he grew accustomed to the feeling of free-falling, Osman began to devise plans for even greater falls. Instead of setting his gear up to catch a fall between five and fifty feet—as would happen in traditional climbing—Osman set up the gear so he would fall between two hundred and eleven hundred feet before being caught by his rope.

Although controlled free-falling resembles bungee jumping or BASE jumping in its conception, it surpasses these in both speed and adrenaline surge. In bungee jumping, the cord attached to the jumper begins to slow the fall about halfway through the drop. In BASE jumping, the parachute is deployed long before the participant reaches maximum velocity. Falling with only a climbing rope attached to his harness, Osman achieved maximum speed and free-fell longer than the other types of jumpers. He would jump from a fixed point above and parallel to his anchor, the point where the rope is attached. When he reached the maximum length of the rope, fixed firmly to his harness, his body would then go into an arcing swing, which he called "flossing the sky."

Support and Criticism

Osman set up many different jumps with climbing ropes, some from bridges and others from rock structures in Yosemite. Always wanting to share his experiences, he encouraged friends to join him in his free-falling endeavors. Osman's rope jumping feats received much support from fellow adrenaline seekers, but they also gained a multitude of critics. Fellow climbers Ron Kauk and Dean Potter recognized Osman's mastery of controlled falling but found it against their nature to let go of the rock to initiate the fall. As Potter says, "I did . . . one jump and I didn't like it. My climbing has always been about control, throwing myself off the rocks like that, thinking maybe I live, maybe I die pretty much freaked me out. But Dano [Osman] was a master at this stuff." [21]

Other critics were not as kind with their words. *Outside* magazine called Osman "really quite stupid" and chastised his sport for its "dubious merits and obvious dangers." [22] Many climbers viewed Osman's jumps as reckless or as fulfilling some sort of death wish. Even more criticism came when a young climber died while replicating one of Osman's jumps from a California bridge. The Yosemite park rangers tried to determine if what Osman was doing violated some established park policy. They had already outlawed BASE jumping in the park, and many felt that this was potentially an even more dangerous sport.

Gaining Notoriety

During the winter of 1996, Dan Osman met Nikki Warren at a local health food restaurant. The two began dating and soon moved in together, along with her daughter Coral. True to his teenage Yosemite days, Osman was still living a hand-to-mouth existence in some ways, although his skill as a carpenter and rope technician landed him a job as safety coordinator for a local high-rise construction job. He also worked as an adjunct professor at the local university teaching climbing techniques. He was often known around Tahoe as the guy who jumps off of stuff.

Osman tests his climbing ropes and anchors before a controlled free fall. Critics chastised Osman for his controversial, free-falling rope jumps.

During this same period, Osman became a member of the North Face climbing team. Through company funding, Osman was able to travel around the world and climb in different locations. He welcomed this return to standard rock climbing for the chance to explore routes that had never been attempted before and to share his experience with some of the world's most renowned climbers. One trip took him to Kyrgyzstan to establish routes on unclimbed mountains with fellow team members Lynn Hill, Jay Smith, and Alex Lowe. His home life was secure, his skills as a carpenter were rewarded, and his place among the world's elite climbers was acknowledged not only through films and magazine ads but as a sponsored professional climber on the North Face team.

Setting Sights Higher

In addition to climbing around the world, Osman continued free-falling greater distances from bridges and fixed objects. Many of his record-breaking jumps were performed in Yosemite. Eric Perlman filmed some of these falls for his *Masters of Stone* videos. They show Osman riding skateboards and bikes off of cliffs, hanging upside down from bridges, and launching into a headfirst free fall. Still more of his record-breaking jumps were done alone or with a small group of friends for the sheer thrill of the fall. Osman kept dreaming of larger jumps and greater falls.

In late October 1998, Osman moved his elaborate anchor system from five hundred feet above Yosemite's valley floor to a position that stood over thirteen hundred feet high. Stretching a rope between the Fifi Buttress and the Rostrum provided more than twice the potential for new record-breaking falls than his previous spot had. Over the course of several days, Osman and friends took more than a dozen jumps on these ropes into the air above Yosemite Valley, adding extra feet with each drop. Their early jumps began with six-hundred-foot falls, but the last jump ended at close to nine hundred feet. With such a great fall, dynamic climbing ropes stretch, bringing the jumpers within just a few hundred feet of the ground.

Unforeseen Arrest Halts Jump

On October 28, Osman returned to Yosemite to break his previous record free fall. However, that morning, Osman was apprehended by the Yosemite park rangers on an outstanding warrant for driving with a suspended license. Although there were not any laws to prevent Osman from rope jumping in the park, they could ensure that he would not jump while in jail.

Osman films the scenery from thousands of feet high during a climbing trip to Kyrgystan. Being an elite, sponsored climber afforded Osman many travel opportunities.

Osman spent the next two weeks in jail, much of that time in solitary confinement. When he was finally released on bail of close to twenty-five thousand dollars, he returned to his sister's house in Reno to await trial. Park rangers also informed him that if he did not retrieve his ropes within a short period of time, they would be confiscated. Just before exploring the full potential of his Yosemite anchor system, he was being forced to dismantle all of his hard work and abandon his dreams.

During his stay in Reno, Osman spent time with Emma and worked on some local construction jobs to fund his upcoming legal battles. In a conversation with friends during this time, Osman acknowledged his love for his daughter and his need to put his adrenaline seeking aside for a while. He said of Emma, "She's the most important fact of my life. Nothing else comes close. . . . I need to give my angels a rest. They've been working overtime keeping me alive, so it's time to put my toys away for a while." [23]

A Return to Yosemite

The call of Yosemite and the desire to retrieve thousands of dollars worth of gear was strong, however, and on November 21, Osman returned to the park with friend and fellow jumper Miles Daisher to break camp and pack up his anchor. The urge to explore the site's potential further proved too great for Osman, and rather than breaking the anchor down, he and Daisher added twenty-five feet to the distance and jumped over nine hundred feet.

Osman carefully free climbs a rock face in Yosemite National Park just weeks before his fatal jumping accident.

Osman neglected to take his anchor down that night, and he and Daisher returned for a final series of jumps in the late afternoon of November 23 to avoid run-ins with the rangers. Daisher made the first jump of the day, with 925 feet of rope, and returned to the top of the tower, where Osman was scrambling to prepare for his greatest jump. It was 5:30 P.M. and darkness was falling along with a light rain.

Realizing that this might be his last jump at this site, Osman felt the need to push his limits further. Daisher describes the scene:

> He'd added 75 feet to the rope, which was about three times more than he usually added from one jump to the next. So he was jumping on a thousand feet of line, which meant he was going to be only about 150 feet off the ground when he stopped. I was really skeptical. I kept saying, "I don't think so, Dano, I don't like this." [24]

Osman's Last Jump

To compensate for the extra length of the rope, Osman picked a new spot to jump from that provided him with more ground clearance. He felt confident about his decision, even though he would not be able to see his untested descent in the dark. Readying for takeoff, he called friends and fellow jumpers Frank Gambalie and Jim Fritsch, who were supposed to be with him but were snowed in at Squaw Valley, California. They listened via cell phone as he made his final countdown for the jump, launched himself off of the cliff, and arced his body against the rapidly approaching ground. Daisher describes what happened next: "In about ten seconds I saw the rope straighten . . . but it didn't make the full whipping sound. Then I heard him yell 'Ahhhhh' and a crash like a tree had broken in half. . . . I yelled to him, got on the radio. Nothing. Quiet." [25]

When Daisher arrived at the cliff's bottom, he saw shattered branches everywhere. Among the broken trees he found the motionless body of Dan Osman, lying at rest on his side. Daisher checked Osman for a pulse, and upon finding none, made calls to the Yosemite ranger station and the friends who had been listening on Osman's phone before impact. He told them that Osman was dead. Friend and fellow climber Dean Potter was called from the search-and-rescue team to come out and keep watch over the body to ward off scavenging bears and coyotes. Dan Osman's dream of the perfect fall had ended in his death at the age of thirty-five.

The Aftermath

A memorial ceremony for Osman was held on November 28, 1998, at his beloved Cave Rock. More than two hundred friends and family members attended the gathering to watch his ashes "floss the skies" over Lake Tahoe. The rope on which his life ended still hung over the chasm between Fifi Buttress and the Rostrum in Yosemite, pending further investigation by park service employees. When it was finally removed weeks later by an anonymous friend and delivered to a climbing rope company for analysis, Osman's fatal mistake was revealed.

Along with the rope that Osman jumped on, there was another rope in the system used to pull the line back up after the jump was finished. By moving to launch himself from a new point, he had inadvertently crossed his jump line over this retrieval line. The sheer force of the thousand feet of his rope sliding across the other line literally disintegrated the cord that held Osman secure above the ground. Just as the rope was supposed to catch Osman and pendulum him across the floor of Yosemite Valley, it was severed by the other line and he went into an uncontrollable free fall into the trees and earth below.

Dan Osman was an amazing climber who excelled at all aspects of the sport. His image is synonymous with overcoming fear and pushing the limits of both body and mind. Videos of his free-solo climbs and rope falls depict his mastery of controlling fear and successfully overcoming seemingly insurmountable obstacles. He will always be remembered as a rock climber and free-faller with strength, determination, and style. Like a true samurai warrior, Osman lived and died by the sword of his own creation, doing what he loved the most, defying gravity and flying freely through the skies.

CHAPTER 3

Kristen Ulmer: Freeskiing Pioneer

Kristen Ulmer is one of the original pioneers of the sport of freeskiing. She is best known for big cliff jumps and first descents down treacherous backcountry slopes. She has also survived five avalanches and several careening cartwheels in areas with dangerous obstacles and great avalanche potential. In 1997 she made the first female descent of Wyoming's Grand Teton, but wondered afterward what all the fuss was about, since several men had already accomplished the descent. While she is proud of her womanhood, Ulmer does not want to be considered merely a female athlete; she is an athlete first and foremost. Repeatedly named in ski industry magazines as a top athlete in her sport, Kristen Ulmer is considered one of the greatest freeskiers in the world.

Growing Up in New Hampshire

Kristen Ulmer was born in Henniker, New Hampshire, on September 8, 1966. Her father, Ed, was a trained concert pianist and a college music professor, while Kristen's mother, Dolores, worked as a nurse. Kristen began skiing at the local mountain, Pat's Peak, at the age of seven. However, she was not initially a natural athlete. In fact, she often found herself picked last for most sports in elementary school.

This did not change when she reached high school. Kristen and her brother Ed Jr. both went to Henniker High School, a small public institution with just over one hundred students. She played junior varsity volleyball there but was never selected to participate in varsity sports. She was on the gymnastics team in her early teens and even played soccer—on the boys team due to a lack of male participants—but she never fully enjoyed team sports.

Although team sports did not appeal to Kristen as a young adult, she was drawn to skiing. Skiing provided an escape from the pressures of fitting in and excelling at standard athletic activities. It also allowed her a chance to progress at her own level, as she basically taught herself the fundamentals of skiing. Joining her high school ski club enabled Kristen to visit larger mountains such as Killington Peak in Vermont, but she mainly honed her skills at her local mountain.

Early Choices

In her early teens, Kristen had begun using drugs. Drugs like alcohol and marijuana made her feel cool, a part of the popular crowd. However, after a time, Kristen found drugs to be a dead end for her natural creativity and motivation. She decided to focus her energy on more positive pursuits instead. Kristen explains the experience:

> I got into drugs and alcohol at an early age. It was very unusual at that time because I was just thirteen. Then, at the age of fourteen, I quit all that. When I did it, though, I did it one hundred percent. So I think I have the tendency in my personality to be an extreme person. Though I was always very aggressive, I wasn't focused. The focus came when I discovered skiing. [26]

Later on, Kristen also found confidence in other avenues. At the age of fifteen, she was elected first runner-up in the Miss Teen New Hampshire competition. At this point, she became more popular with her peers, mostly for being a pretty girl in a small town. While the newfound attention was exciting in some ways, as time went on, Kristen began to realize that much of her success in life was based on physical attributes: her looks and her growing ability to ski. This realization led her to search for other outlets of expression, and she filled this void by taking standard college classes in her early teens at the local university where her father taught. Education became a lifelong passion for Kristen both in the classroom and on the slopes.

As a skier, Kristen was mainly self-taught. The few training sessions she had with a coach brought her to the point of tears, as he pressured her too hard to perform. She decided that it was more beneficial for her to push herself, rather than seek external support and guidance. Skiing had been her means of self-expression, and sharing that experience with a coach was not helping her progress.

Moving to the Big Mountains

Ulmer graduated from high school at age seventeen in 1984. She took classes at the University of New Hampshire for a while. However, in 1987, at the age of twenty, Ulmer moved to Salt Lake City, Utah, to focus on her skiing full-time. She began competing local-

Kristen Ulmer's determination, drive, and fearlessness on the mountain helped her to become one of the world's top female freeskiers.

ly in mogul competitions (moguls are bumps in ski runs) and wanted more than anything to make a career out of skiing. Though Ulmer was quite a strong skier even at this time, she did not perform very well in these early competitions. While she had a strong dedication to skiing and training, Ulmer still found that she was holding herself back, unable to fully unleash her potential due to unresolved personal issues centered around beauty, popularity, and her ability to ski.

Already on the verge of becoming a world-class skier, Ulmer decided to first spend some quality time reflecting on her life and goals. She credits a five-month solo trip to Asia in 1988 with giving her the confidence and motivation necessary to become a champion. She says of the trip,

> I made myself as ugly as possible, and my rule was I wasn't allowed to talk about skiing when I met people. . . . I kept a journal and didn't take any photos, so I wouldn't come back from the trip and say, "Look at me, look what I've done." It was a completely personal thing. It had the biggest impact on my life of anything I've ever done. I came back really inwardly confident. . . . The next winter I basically went from an expert skier to a world-class skier. [27]

Ulmer came back from her journey with a newfound focus. She dedicated all of her energy to the goal of becoming a professional skier. Through sheer determination and training, within a few months she emerged as a world-class skier. Her time was spent competing in traditional ski runs set on a plotted course. Before her trip, she held back during competition, but after her return, she began opening up, speeding through bumpy mogul runs at breakneck speeds. In 1991 Kristen Ulmer qualified for the U.S. mogul team, amazing the ski community with her ability to power through steep, treacherous terrain. This form of skiing has been an Olympic sport for nearly a century, and in order to compete, one must qualify for his or her country's ski team.

Meanwhile, Ulmer also won the Extreme Mogul National Championships in Crested Butte, Colorado, in 1992, which was separate from her mogul competitions on the U.S. team. Though she loved the opportunity to participate on the U.S. ski team, there were two major factors that detracted from her experience as a competitive athlete. First, Ulmer was one of the few professional skiers who did not come from a wealthy family. Ski team members were expected to pay their own way on trips and cover their entry fees. At the same time, they were not allowed to accept money via endorsements from sponsors or film deals, because they had to solely represent the U.S. ski team's sponsors. Second, Ulmer's busy competition schedule

Ulmer carves a turn during a high-speed, downhill run in Utah. Dedicated to becoming a professional skier, Ulmer moved to Utah in 1987 to ski full-time.

Ulmer clears a dangerous rock section while jumping down a steep run near Snowbasin, Utah.

and constant pressure to perform took its toll on her body. She explains her feelings at the time:

> I was basically on the U.S. ski team and I was also being called the best overall woman extreme skier in the world by all the magazines. . . . I didn't ski a day where I wasn't either being judged, coached, filmed, or photographed. . . . They would announce my name and everyone would recognize me from the films and from being an extreme skier. . . . My ego was

also wrapped up in my extreme skiing. Because I spent so much time skiing for films in between mogul competitions, and I hadn't been training for moguls, I never competed for the U.S. ski team well, and it was embarrassing to me and frustrating. I just wasn't focused on mogul skiing. I was focused on filming and so . . . I was so burnt out I blew my knee out.[28]

Grappling with knee injuries and undergoing multiple surgeries left Ulmer wondering if her body could continue to withstand the constant abuse of professional skiing.

Choosing Freeskiing

After her initial knee injury healed at the end of 1992, Ulmer did not return to mogul skiing but chose to focus exclusively on extreme freeskiing. Freeskiing involves navigating backcountry runs, overcoming natural obstacles, and often jumping or dropping long distances. The hazards involved in freeskiing are often unavoidable, including falling in no-fall zones where, if one crashes, rocks, cliffs, and avalanches guarantee injury, if not death.

While Ulmer excelled at both forms of skiing, she chose the freeskiing discipline over moguls for reasons related to health, income, and notoriety. Even though she would eventually go on to launch front flips off of cliffs more than thirty feet high and navigate terrain with high avalanche potential, the wear and tear of repeatedly skiing the bumps of moguls at top speed was still more debilitating on her body. Through freeskiing, she was also able to make a considerable income and accept the support of sponsors in the form of cash and free gear.

During this time, Ulmer began appearing in several extreme skiing films. Her first appearances were in four RAP (Real Action Pictures) films and five North Face Extreme Team movies. These films show Ulmer navigating steep, obstacle-ridden terrain and launching off of cliffs with deft precision. She makes seemingly impossible feats look commonplace as she negotiates her way down the mountain. She says about making ski films, "They are really dangerous to film. Unless you are risking your life, you usually don't make it into a movie. . . . Unless you're willing to go out there and put your body and your life on the line it's not filmworthy."[29] She next appeared in two Teton Gravity Research films, including the film *Uprising*.

Ulmer became the poster child for extreme skiing, noted as one of the only women in a predominately male-dominated sport. She explains freeskiing's lure:

I found I really liked the danger . . . putting my neck out there and somehow surviving. As I became a better skier, I began taking bigger and bigger risks. . . . Those athletes who hang their neck out the farthest . . . get the most sponsorship money, film jobs, and publicity. . . . I've struggled my whole life to execute flips or tear through steep trees at breakneck speed, because that's what it took to ski like a man, to satiate my own internal drive, and to be taken seriously. [30]

Ulmer wanted to be the best skier period, regardless of gender. "I've never promoted myself as a woman athlete," she says. "I am just an athlete period, and I think that is why I have been successful. . . . Just be an athlete and be incredible, and stop drawing attention to the fact that you are black or white or male or female, and then people will stop seeing it that way." [31] Regardless of gender or color, Kristen Ulmer had become one of the top freeskiers in the world.

Driven by Excitement

Always yearning for adventure and travel, Ulmer went to Valdez, Alaska, in 1995 to ski remote backcountry mountains that are accessible only by helicopter. After nine days of bad weather not suitable for skiing, she became bored and decided to leave. In Alaska, hitchhiking is common, so Ulmer did not think twice about catching a ride to the heliport with a stranger. After driving some distance, the man threatened to rape and kill her. Despite the very dangerous situation, though, Ulmer was able to stay calm. She explains her thoughts at the time:

My first reaction when he started going off on me was, thank God, something interesting is finally happening to me. . . . What I did was show a nonchalant . . . attitude toward him while he was screaming. I wasn't giving him a power trip . . . I just made small talk with him while he was screaming at me. When women aren't totally frightened, it's no fun for a rapist. So I just decided I wasn't going to be scared of him. [32]

The man eventually pulled the van over and let Ulmer out, adding one more story to her list of dangers overcome, even though this one was not on the mountain.

The Teton Descent

The trip to Alaska had been exciting for reasons other than skiing. But in her subsequent trips there, hopes of skiing first descents were often foiled by bad weather. Though her passion and dedication to skiing had earned her the reputation as the best, most spectacular, and craziest female skier in three of the top ski industry magazines, Ulmer yearned for a greater challenge. She continued to ski incredibly hard backcountry runs both on camera and as a means of personal fulfillment, but she also set her sights on a new goal.

Kristen Ulmer first attempted to ski Wyoming's Grand Teton in early 1997 with good friend and fellow skier Tom Jungst and professional mountaineer Alex Lowe. Although the thirteen-thousand-foot-plus peak had been skied before by her male contemporaries, no woman had ever attempted the perilous descent. Ulmer first attempted to climb the mountain and then ski down. According to Ulmer, "I'm really an avid climber, so to combine my two favorite sports increases the challenge. . . . The first time I tried to ski the Grand Teton, we were so exhausted before we ever reached the top that I thought there's no way I'm going to have the strength to focus and ski . . . down a forty-five to fifty degree slope on what is typically very bad snow." [33] Just over a thousand feet from the summit, Ulmer, Jungst, and Lowe decided to turn back due to high avalanche risk and fatigue.

Unwilling to let her dream die, Ulmer returned to the Grand Teton on June 8, 1997, and became the first woman to ever ski the treacherous mountain. Although many of her turns sent off avalanches, she stayed focused and alert on the descent, successfully completing her run, which included waiting four hours for the avalanche activity to stop. Looking back on the feat, she admits that the conditions were definitely not optimal:

> I think we went a little overboard, but I was absolutely determined to ski the Grand Teton. Once I get my mind set on something . . . I do it. The pressure to do it came from myself, and on the practical side, I knew it would be huge for my career. . . . If the risk is greater than the reward, I have no problem walking away. I won't lose sleep over it. But at the same time, I know how happy I'll be after I accomplish it. [34]

Developing a Writing Career

Being the only female to ski the Grand Teton elevated Ulmer from a celebrity to near ski goddess status. Magazines that had already taken note of her ability to ski moguls, negotiate jumps, and land perfectly on difficult terrain now showered her with compliments and awards. *Powder* magazine called her the biggest icon the ski industry never expected; *Conde Nast Sports for Women* deemed her the most extreme female athlete in the country; and *Skiing* magazine asked her to join its staff, writing a feature article for every issue.

Although she had written off and on for years, the position at *Skiing* magazine gave Ulmer a forum for her unique perspective on the ski industry and life in general. She soon began publishing articles in other ski magazines as well.

Ulmer was quite productive during this time period, appearing in several more ski documentaries and completing an international politics degree at the University of Utah. Her schedule was also filled with deadlines for her articles as well as interviews for other magazines. As one example of her new popularity outside of ski industry magazines, *Elle* magazine called Ulmer one of "America's best bodies" in the February 1999 issue.

Ulmer hikes up a steep, snow-covered mountain trail with her skis and gear in tote. In 1997 Ulmer became the first woman ever to ski down Wyoming's treacherous Grand Teton run.

Ulmer's renown was not limited to the pages of magazines. She also got the chance to host an international extreme sports show called *The Edge,* which ran for roughly a year in 1999. Although the show was a fun experience for her, she received very little payment for her time and work on the project. It did, however, help to spread her fame as an extreme skier beyond the boundaries of North America.

A Frightening Experience

Growing international exposure led to one of Ulmer's most frightening experiences. In early May 2000, she took a trip to Chamonix, France, to join fellow freeskiers Stephane "Fan Fan" Dan and Nicolas Mermoud from France and Francine Moreillon of Switzerland in navigating the steep couloirs of Mont Blanc for an article in *Skiing.* Couloirs are tight, avalanche-prone ski runs on incredibly steep (fifty- to seventy-degree) slopes. Usually May is a good month for skiing couloirs, because the snowpack is more stable and predictable, but that particular year the avalanche potential, due to a recent storm, had become high.

The mountain conditions were good in the morning, but as the sun hit, certain slope conditions deteriorated rapidly. After negotiating the top of their chosen couloirs, the group found themselves huddled beneath a buttress on the wall of a seventy-degree slope when the avalanches began. The first small avalanches blew right past, down a chute five feet to the right of them, but as the sun warmed the slopes above, the avalanches grew bigger and faster, until they were on top of them. Ulmer describes the experience:

> The slope was too steep and icy to take a step in any direction.... I had only inch-deep chips in the white ice to stand on.... The slides kept getting bigger ... and then the big one came.... I have never imagined anything so loud, violent, fast, or crushing. I sucked a quick breath and lay flat for 20 seconds, waiting for the beating to end, then slowly stood back up and shook away the snow caked around me. ... All I could do was take quick, scared breaths in, like a drowning fish.... How on earth could we have survived that? It was seven stories high.[35]

Shortly after the huge wave of snow nearly swept the group off the slope, a rescue helicopter arrived. Surprised to see the four skiers still living, the pilot lowered a basket to retrieve each member of the group. At the time of the incident, Ulmer made no comment, but, nearly a year later, she wrote an article titled "Cliffhanger" for *Skiing* that described the experience. Although she had had several scary falls in the past, cartwheeling momentarily on no-fall zones before making a life-or-death recovery and surviving several avalanches, this couloir on Mont Blanc was the closest she came to death in her career as a professional skier. The experience made her realize that being a professional risk taker was actually quite silly.

Searching for a Life Apart

Realizing that she would not be able to perform death-defying ski stunts for the rest of her life, Ulmer chose to explore other avenues to share her extreme experiences. She continued writing for *Skiing* magazine throughout 2001, and published articles in other magazines such as *Powder, Freeze,* and *Penthouse.* She tried her hand at public speaking at motivational seminars and ski industry workshops, but found that writing was more her medium than speech. After years of basing success on extreme skiing, Ulmer felt as if she needed to experience different aspects of life. Part of her wanted to drop everything that defined her life at the moment and return to school for a law degree, but she thought that decision would be a waste of her natural talent as a professional athlete.

Wanting to share her experience with the rest of the world, Ulmer chose to focus her energy on organizing a personal growth ski workshop that appealed to professional skiers and newcomers alike. The result was a mountain workshop called "Ski to Live." She describes the workshop in a letter to *Skier's Journal:*

> The goal in Ski to Live will be to learn about who we are as people through the sport of skiing . . . by joining your ski day with wellness workshops and seminars. . . . We will help you reach into your mind and body to discover what kind of skier and person you were meant to be. . . . Our objective: to help people with their passion and purpose in life, while reveling in the wonders of skiing and the camaraderie of great people.[36]

The first two Ski to Live workshops went so well that Ulmer decided to continue to pursue this new interest. The seminars enabled her to share her exciting lifestyle and knowledge of skiing with a variety of individuals while allowing the guests to explore the meaning of sports and adventure in their own lives. By hiring a spiritual leader and other ski and snowboard coaches to work alongside her, Ulmer has created a means for both herself and others to gain personal insight.

Ulmer fearlessly free-falls from a high cliff in Utah. While still occasionally performing death-defying stunts, Ulmer focuses more on her writing projects and public seminars.

Ulmer currently lives in Salt Lake City, Utah, where she skis and climbs. Her recent summers have been spent in Hood River, Oregon, kiteboarding on the Columbia River. She continues to ski incredibly extreme slopes and writes frequently for many international publications. Over the course of her career, she has excelled at both traditional and freestyle ski competitions, sharing her experiences with the rest of the world through her many films and magazine articles. One statement made by Kristen Ulmer defines her view of life: "Go big. That's a reference to doing a big jump and catching big air, but it applies to everyday life, too. I talk about the importance of going big in whatever you do. . . . Don't do it halfway."[37]

CHAPTER 4

Tao Berman: The Art of Extreme Paddling

Tao Berman has taken the sport of white-water kayaking, or paddling, to new extremes with his bold and daring descents of extremely dangerous rapids. He has excelled at all forms of kayaking, but Berman especially loves steep, narrow, tight rivers with an abundance of waterfalls to drop. He has pushed the levels of extreme kayaking to new highs with his bold first descents down rapids and waterfalls deemed impassable and beyond any white-water rating system. Even before achieving international notoriety as an extreme paddler, Berman was navigating his kayak down some of the most demanding rivers in the world.

Growing Up in the Woods

Born on January 28, 1979, in Washington's Northern Cascade mountains, Tao Berman did not lead an average lifestyle growing up. His father, Birch Berman, was a backcountry hiking guide, and his mother was a massage therapist. On one of her trips to Africa, a medicine man gave Tao's mother the name Silver Moon, and she went by it from then after. His family, which included an older sister, Lilly, and younger brother, Osho, also led a rugged life. Throughout his childhood, Tao lived in a small house nestled in the mountains that had no running water, electricity, or indoor plumbing. Some children would consider this upbringing hard, but Tao looks back on it fondly: "It doesn't get any better than my childhood. I spent my years riding my bike up and down mountains, climbing up trees and jumping from one to another twenty to thirty feet up in the air, probably living out every kid's dream. It was awesome." [38]

Tao's parents separated when he was about four, and in 1989, Tao moved with his mother, brother, and sister to the Seattle suburb of Monroe, Washington. Even though they gained the amenities of electricity and indoor plumbing, Tao never lost his love of the outdoors and the curiosity to push his limits within that realm. He constantly rode bikes and skied in the local Cascade mountains, often injuring himself in the process. Unwilling to give up, he would think of ways to perfect his performance in order to avoid future mishaps.

Early Outdoor Pursuits

Tao's rustic upbringing had introduced him to outdoor adventure sports, and he began rock climbing and kayaking at the age of fourteen. At the time, he was also a wrestler on his middle school team, but he gave up the sport when high school coaches began scouting him. He explains his choice: "I was really good at wrestling, and the high school coach was watching me and was like, 'I'm going to make you one of the best. You're going to start training six days a week.' I said, 'Wait a minute.' I was kayaking, climbing, skiing . . . I wasn't willing to give up all of those just for one sport." [39]

Tao chose to continue his outdoor pursuits, but began focusing on kayaking at the age of fifteen. One of his early training grounds was Washington's Skykomish River, which was commercially run by rafting companies. Tao worked as a raft guide in the summers, gaining experience at reading and navigating advanced white water. During this time, he paddled the same river in his kayak, developing his fundamental skills. He describes why he chose to paddle over all other pursuits:

> I chose kayaking because I knew that the only limit in kayaking would be one that I would set for myself. I wanted a sport with a high level of risk. Something where there is no middle ground. Either you succeed or fail. I knew kayaking would make me the best that I could be. Kayaking is also something that I can do for myself without relying on others. My successes and failures are my own. [40]

Tao did succeed at paddling, and this success made him eager to finish school early, so he could have more time to kayak. Tao enrolled in an Advance Placement program that enabled him to gain college credit at a nearby community college in Everett, Washington, while still taking classes at Monroe High School. He also began pushing his limits at boating during this time, testing his skills on some of the steep, narrow creeks that flowed abundantly throughout the Cascade mountains.

Though he did not realize it at the time, Tao was kayaking at the same level as some of the world's top paddlers. His initiation to boating was on steep creeks, and he was forced to learn fast or suffer long, frightening swims. Although he was unaware of the fact, some of the rapids he ran were first descents—that is, previously unnavigated runs.

Tao Berman began kayaking as a teenager and immediately tested the limits of what was thought possible in the sport.

Tao describes his early experiences with extreme paddling: "There was all kinds of first descent stuff to do up in Washington State, and I immediately started pushing what could be done. I started to set first descents not realizing how difficult they were relative to what other professionals were doing out there in the world just because I was doing my own thing in the Northwest." [41]

Time Off to Paddle

Tao Berman graduated from high school in 1997, but rather than going straight to college, he chose to take a year off and paddle full-time. He wanted to explore new rivers and try to push his limits at extreme kayaking before he had to focus on school once again. This journey took him to many different destinations in Mexico, and it also put him on the map as one of the world's most extreme paddlers.

While in the state of Veracruz, Mexico, Berman navigated his kayak over what could be called the biggest waterfall drop ever, on

Berman navigates his kayak down a dangerous waterfall in British Columbia. At just eighteen years old, Berman was already kayaking at a professional level.

the El Tomato River. Fellow boater and videographer Christian Knight describes the waterfall: "The eighty-three foot waterfall . . . was swollen from the recent hurricane that ripped through Mexico, littering the river, as well as the country with garbage. The water was thick, brown, and unpredictable. More significantly, the water-fall was nestled deep in a treacherous canyon farther away from civilization than most people would prefer to go." [42]

After dropping the falls, Berman disappeared into the swirling vortex below, rolling his capsized kayak upright seconds later. Unintentionally, Berman had dropped one of the largest falls ever attempted in a kayak. However, the *Guinness Book of World Records* did not recognize it as such due to improper documentation. It was, however, recorded on video by Eric Link in his 1999 kayaking film called *Twitch*. Link is one of the premier white-water videographers, and many of his films include footage of Berman. Most paddlers acknowledged Berman's drop as a world record despite *Guinness's* views otherwise.

After this descent, Tao Berman's name began circulating within the worldwide paddling community as a person to watch. This new-found attention made Berman realize that he was paddling at a level that few other boaters dreamed possible, running rapids that even experienced paddlers shied away from. Several companies began sponsoring Berman during this time as well, including Stohlquist WaterWare, Werner Paddles, and Dagger Kayaks. With this support, he entered the world of professional paddling before ever attending college.

When Berman returned to the United States from Mexico in 1998, he decided to enroll in college. Drawn to the abundance of paddling opportunities nearby, he moved to Arcata, California, and attended Humbolt State university there. He attended the school for only a semester because he did not like the town of Arcata. Relocating to nearby Ashland, Oregon, he enrolled into Southern Oregon university there to study business and marketing. During this time, Berman continued to devote all of his free time to paddling, focusing more on that aspect of his life than his studies.

World-Record Waterfall

Always interested in new challenges, Berman began dreaming of bigger falls to drop in his kayak. He exhausted many of the possibilities around the Oregon and Washington area, but found what he was looking for during the shooting of Eric Link's *Twitch 2000* film in Canada during the summer of 1999. With Link and other members of the *Twitch* video production team, Berman set about exploring remote areas of Banff National Park. Much of their journey brought them mosquito bites, twisted ankles, and tired muscles from their bushwhacking through uncharted river gorges in the heat of summer. Finally, on August 23, 1999, tired but not defeated, Berman found a huge waterfall with a seven-foot-wide opening at the top. The upper walls were rocky and narrow, and a large rock jutted out toward the water at the bottom of the cascading flume. Christian Knight describes the discovery:

> It was a dramatic waterfall. . . . Tao knew then it would be another world record, and this time there would be no disputing it. . . . This one in particular seemed to have an undeniable pull at Tao. . . . It was not the perfect waterfall. Things could happen in a few seconds that could change his life forever. To live in a world surrounded by regret would be an awful thing. This is the tragedy of Tao's mind. That is why he can't just simply walk away. There is only one way for him to elude that awful world, and that is to run it, whatever it is, an unrunnable rapid, or the world record waterfall and run it clean. [43]

Berman scouted the rapid from above and below, gathering a number of onlookers in the process. As he circled the water above the falls, some onlookers cheered while others averted their eyes in fear and horror. Some friends even thought of ways to deter him from running the 98.4-foot drop such as taking his paddle or helmet away from him, but Berman would not be deterred. Knight looked to the top of the falls and saw Berman give a thumbs-up; he had definitely chosen to drop the falls. Berman put two milk jugs full of water 'in the nose of his kayak to ensure a vertical entry into the water at the bottom of the falls, donned extra protective gear to avoid abrasions and head injury, and positioned himself back in his boat, poised to make the drop of his life.

Berman paddled through the narrow corridor and entered the falls. After an eighty-foot free fall, he brushed against a rock with his shoulder, but still managed to land in the pool below. He describes the world-record drop and its aftermath:

> I was moving at about 55 miles per hour for about 2.4 seconds, so if I landed flat, it would have been like a car crash. I had to be very vertical in my kayak and then lean over the front to be as aerodynamic into the water as possible to try to minimize the impact that it would have on my body. . . . After landing, I flexed all my muscles to make sure I wasn't

Berman scouts the landing zone of "Corndog Falls," along Washington's Snoqualmie River. Berman's dramatic waterfall drop of 98.4 feet at Banff National Park was officially recognized as a world record.

injured. . . . The first thing was, "Am I OK?" Then I rolled back up with half of a paddle blade. Half my paddle blade broke off on impact. To give you an idea of how big a hit that is, my paddle takes about 840 pounds of pressure to break. So I busted the paddle and hit very hard. . . . I woke up the next day and felt like I had been hit by a train. My whole body was sore, but nothing was injured at all.[44]

International Recognition

This time, Berman's drop was officially recognized by the *Guinness Book of World Records* as the longest waterfall descent ever taken in a kayak. Berman was immediately thrust into the limelight among extreme paddling figures. While he already had multiple sponsors and a variety of filmed first descents to his credit, Berman now had many offers to endorse various products or appear in certain videos. At this point, Berman was able to support himself solely from kayaking.

Berman returned to school in the fall, but found it hard to concentrate on his studies and focus on his career as a professional paddler at the same time. One incident that helped him decide to quit school came when the television show *Ripley's Believe It or Not* had to film him in class due to time constraints. Berman explains his decision to quit college and focus on his career:

> I had to choose between my paddling career and college. . . .
> I'm not going to do two things at sixty or seventy percent. I
> want to do one as good as I can. . . . I love what I do. I love
> the business side of what I do. I love the marketing side of
> what I do. If there's something I want to learn about, I'll go
> to a bookstore and get a book, so at this point, I don't see
> going back to college.[45]

Freestyle Success

Not wanting to be typecast as just an extreme paddler performing harebrained stunts as eye candy for video viewers, Berman decided to focus on a different aspect of his sport: freestyle paddling. Freestyle kayaking differs from extreme paddling in that it takes place at a set spot on a river within a feature known as a hole, a swirling vortex of white water located above a natural obstacle such as a rock. Paddlers enter the hole and perform a series of tricks within its clutches for a set amount of time. The moves are given a point rating by judges, and the paddler with the highest amount of points wins the competition. While this form of paddling is not as extreme as first descents over high waterfalls, it does require precise skill to perform. Although Berman did not qualify for the U.S. freestyle kayak team in 1999, he succeeded in 2000, joining the elite group of professional freestyle paddlers representing the United States in international kayaking competitions.

Setting New Records

While freestyle paddling, Berman still remained true to his first love: extreme boating. He made two more record-breaking first descents within a twenty-four-hour period in the year 2000. He broke the speed-altitude descent record on May 15 by dropping one hundred feet over a five-waterfall stretch on a tributary to Washington's Snoqualmie River in 19.38 seconds. The very next day, on a tributary to the Carbon River in Washington, Berman broke the vertical distance descent record by dropping over 210 feet along a one-eighth-of-a-mile stretch of rapids. He says of his ability to perform such extreme descents, "If I can't visualize every detail of what I'm about to do, I'll get out of my kayak. There's no time for fear or doubt. That would slow my reaction time, which would be catastrophic." [46]

For Berman, a drop, no matter how hard, is based on precise calculations and planning. As Knight says, "Tao lives in a world where his actions are limited only by what he thinks he cannot predict. The inevitable prospect of death can be removed by a graceful combination of skill and precise calculation; however, if he cannot remove the probability of death or serious injury, then he reluctantly removes himself." [47]

Berman continued to search out rapids and falls with known obstacles. Filming another *Twitch* video on the Top Tye River in Washington, he ran a thirty-foot falls that was previously deemed unrunnable because of two huge trees in the middle of it. Always eager to achieve the "impossible," Berman scouted the falls closely before paddling over it. He launched off of a rock at the top of the falls, catching enough air to land on one of the trees, standing near vertical in the middle of the drop. Balancing his kayak, he then slid down the tree, much like

Berman spins a cartwheel in his freestyle kayak on Oregon's Lake Creek. Freestyle paddling allowed Berman to expand beyond the sport's extreme modes.

skateboarders slide along railings, and dropped into the pool below, successfully completing the first descent.

Several days later Berman returned to the same falls at higher water levels to attempt the drop for the cameras again, but he miscalculated his landing and was unable to balance on the tree. He fell off the side onto a shelf, but managed to exit the boat and stand on the shelf before being swept down the next falls. Berman recounts the experience:

> I am very confident in my ability to be successful. I don't believe that running drops is about surviving. It's about running a drop and looking good doing it. For that reason I have had very few close calls. . . . I knew before running the drop that that was a possibility, so I checked out the consequences before running the drop and decided that it was still worth doing.[48]

Close Calls in Calm Water

Another close call came for Berman, ironically, on an easy section of Idaho's Lochsa River. While spinning on a rock, a routine maneuver in freestyle kayaking, he capsized and was sucked under the water. Pinned between his kayak and the rock, Berman tried to extricate himself but found his leg stuck with the force of all the water pushing on it. Thinking quickly, he got back into the boat and used his arms to pull his leg free. Once entirely out of the boat, he had to choose which way to swim: One way would lead to the surface and safety, while the other would go farther under the rock and lead to almost certain death by drowning.

Thinking rationally, Berman looked for some source of light, and upon finding it, pushed in that direction, finally breaking the surface of the water. He recalls his thoughts of the experience:

> It's funny for me. I look back at that whole experience and the only thing that was scary about it for me was that I thought it was so much fun. I was stuck under this rock, and granted I wouldn't go back and do it again, but after popping up, I was thinking, "Man, that was so cool." I was thinking about how my brain was working and I was just so mellow under the rock. . . . I should have been a lot more scared or a bit shaken up, but I wasn't. I think for me the experience was just more insight into the type of personality that I have. I just love putting it all on the line and having to keep a real level head and do whatever I'm doing the best I can to make it.[49]

Winning the Pre-Worlds

Not letting his brushes with injury and death deter him from his desire to perform, Berman continued to focus mainly on first descents down extreme white water. He has completed more than fifty first descents over the course of his career as an extreme kayaker. Although he did not compete on the U.S. freestyle team in 2001, he did return to the team in 2002, winning the Pre-Worlds Championships in Graz, Austria. This competition is held in the same location a year before the world championships to work out any problems with the contest site.

While Berman excels at freestyle boating, dropping waterfalls and running steep creeks is his first love. He puts his life on the line for extreme paddling, not for the monetary rewards, but for the satisfaction he gains from setting goals and achieving them. According to Berman, "I love extreme kayaking because it pushes me. I know that I am putting it all on the line. . . . It forces me to be the best that I can be. My first love is extreme paddling, but I do freestyle because I enjoy it. It's not a side of my career that brings in much money, but I participate in it for love of the sport." [50]

To the surprise of few, Berman's complete dedication to the sport of kayaking during the last decade has earned him the mark of a true professional. Freelance photographer and Rippin Productions company founder Jock Bradley describes his experiences working with and filming Berman:

> I've found him to be a consummate professional. At the top of a waterfall we will talk about his line. If he needs to change his body or boat position to enhance the shot, then it's done. I have photographed him running some of the most incredible whitewater imaginable. Much of it, where if he were to be off line by six inches he could die. Never once have I questioned his judgment on whether or not something is runnable. Tao has not exhibited Kodak courage, just because there is a photographer . . . nearby. Though youthful in age, his wisdom, maturity, professionalism, and skills extend well beyond his years. [51]

Sharing the Experience

By the year 2002, Berman thrived on his sponsorship income alone. Along with his original sponsors, he had acquired endorsements from Teva sandals, Red Bull energy drinks, and Oakley sunglasses.

Berman runs a steep waterfall along the Cheakamus River in 2003. Despite the risks, Berman continues to test himself on the world's most dangerous waterways.

These companies paid Berman a salary to use his image to endorse their products.

Another aspect of Berman's career consists of public speaking and motivational seminars. Though lecturing to business gatherings brings better pay, he is drawn more to speaking in public schools, where he shares his experiences with young adults. Berman says,

> I'd like to set up a sports foundation to help kids find some positive influence in their lives, find something to be passionate about. I believe a lot of the reason that kids are getting into drugs and making poor choices is because they don't have positive influences around them. If I could create opportunities for children to have those positive choices I don't believe that we would have to lecture them about what not to do. They would already have something positive that they would want to do. [52]

Tao Berman currently lives in Seattle, Washington, and he spends a few months training in Eugene, Oregon, during the winter. He still holds the world records for the highest waterfall drop, the fastest speed-altitude descent, and the longest vertical distance for kayaking. Berman continues to push the limits of extreme kayaking, scouting new, bigger drops for the future. Although the records do not mean as much to him as the personal satisfaction of accomplishing his goals, he is still proud of the niche his accomplishments have carved for him at the top of his profession. "I want to choose the most dangerous routes so if somebody tries to beat the records, they'll need to be fearless and talented," he says. "I don't want easy records." [53]

CHAPTER 5

Glenn Singleman: BASE-Jumping Visionary

Glenn Singleman is one of Australia's most extreme athletes, accomplishing world-record feats in his first year as a BASE jumper. BASE jumping is parachuting from fixed objects with a single canopy or chute that is kept in a pack on the jumper's back. BASE stands for Building, Antenna, Span (bridges), Earth (cliffs), the four different types of objects jumpers launch themselves off of. After roughly a year of training, Glenn Singleman traveled to Pakistan's Great Trango Tower and hurled himself from its vertical cliff at 19,300 feet, becoming the first man to ever attempt, let alone succeed at, jumping from such a height. Singleman documented this feat, as well as other extreme pursuits, on film to share his experience with the rest of the world.

A Strong Work Ethic

Glenn Singleman was born in Sydney, Australia, on October 12, 1958, to parents Elizabeth and Harold Singleman. The two divorced shortly after Glenn's birth, leaving Elizabeth to support Glenn and his older brother, David, on her own. Glenn and David kept their father's last name and visited him frequently. An engineer by trade, Harold Singleman had a passion for the ocean and sailing, which he shared with his sons, instilling in them a love of adventure at an early age.

Without the income and support of a husband, Elizabeth worked quite hard to put her children through twelve years of private education at Trinity Grammar. Glenn remembers his school years with mixed emotions:

> The school that she sent me to was a very strict religious school so I got a lot of good old-fashioned . . . discipline with a capital D. . . . If it's one thing that I attribute to the successes I have had it's that passion for learning and that passion for achieving goals that you set for yourself, and that came from that kind of background at school. In ret-

rospect, I was pleased that I got that formal discipline and formal structure. [54]

While in school, Glenn participated in many sports and greatly enjoyed athletics. He not only swam but played soccer, tennis, and cricket for his school teams.

Record-breaking BASE jumper Glenn Singleman reflects after filming his latest BASE-jumping experience.

Aside from focusing on athletics, Glenn also put a great deal of time into his studies. In Australia, a student's school performance and final exams determine what courses he or she will be able to take at the university level. Glenn focused hard on his studies and did quite well on his final exam, so he was able to pursue medicine as a career at the University of Sydney.

Singleman found medical school to be incredibly demanding. Along with the stress of school, he also had to work a variety of odd jobs during this time to support himself. His days were spent studying and attending classes and labs, while his weekends were filled working as a wine waiter, a factory hand, a car detailer, and even a bartender in a discotheque. Singleman had little time for any other activities aside from work and school, and he found himself yearning to break free and explore the world outside of a textbook.

First Expedition

In 1979, after two years of this schedule, Singleman took a year off from school to visit South America and hike the Gringo Trail in the Andes mountains. This trip was his introduction to extreme trekking, as many sections of the trail required bushwhacking and orienteering over poorly-defined trails. The experience marked the beginning of his lifelong love of adventurous pursuits in the outdoors. After this South American expedition, the treks he did got harder and steeper, leading eventually to climbing and then mountaineering.

After his year of adventuring, Singleman returned to finish his schooling in 1980. It was an intense period of time filled with work and study, and he had no opportunities to travel. After his graduation from medical school, Singleman went straight into his residency in a local hospital. He felt like the last few years of school and the first years of work were much like slave labor: long hours for little pay while he learned his way around the operating room. This was a hard time for Singleman, because being a doctor was not exactly what he expected it to be:

> I came to understand that medicine as a body of knowledge is astounding and wonderful . . . but medicine as a job is very linear nowadays. There is no room for creativity. There is no room for human emotion in it. You have to be detached, scientific . . . and I found it to be somewhat limiting to my creative side. I always had a very strong creative side, but I never had time to do much about that because I was always working full-time. [55]

Following Creative Dreams

During this period, Singleman continued to pursue his love of the outdoors by hiking, climbing, and canyoning in the Blue Mountains surrounding Sydney on three sides. These canyons were formed some 140 million years ago, and some of the structures are over six hundred feet deep with five- to ten-foot-wide paths and creeks along the bottom. These outdoor experiences influenced Singleman to pursue a more creative lifestyle. He wanted to combine his love of the outdoors and his new passion for canyoning, climbing, and trekking with a more creative outlet to express this passion.

In 1985 Singleman enrolled in film school at the University of Technology in Sydney. He spent his weekends working as a doctor and his weekdays and nights attending classes and shooting films. His first postgraduate student film, titled *A Spire,* documented one man's climbing ascent of the tallest building in the Southern Hemisphere, Sydney's Centerpoint Tower. The film was shot over six months in 1987, and it brought Singleman instant recognition in the adventure-film community. In 1988 he sold the movie for twenty-five thousand dollars to a local broadcasting company, proving that his choice to attend film school was not a frivolous one. Singleman describes another reason why he chose to pursue film over medicine:

> I've been able to combine my love of the outdoors with going on expeditions, and whenever I've gone . . . I'm usually involved in the filmmaking and I'm a doctor. . . . I discovered early on that the expedition doctor usually doesn't get paid, but the camera guy always does. So that was another motivator to do camera [work] when I went to film school.[56]

Singleman's background in film and medicine and his knowledge of the outdoors made him a natural asset on any expedition. He continued to make films over the next few years, including one titled *The Loneliest Mountain* in 1988 about an Australian team's attempt at a first ascent of Mount Minto in Antarctica. On this trip, he was able to combine his early love of sailing with his newfound passion for film. He also worked as a cameraman on Leo Dickinson's 1991 film documenting the first hot-air-balloon trip over Mount Everest. Singleman's decision to follow his passion for film led him to many beautiful places throughout the world.

Meeting New People

While climbing Russia's Mount Elbrus in 1991, Singleman met a woman from St. Petersburg named Irina Tolkounora, and the two were immediately attracted to each other. She returned to Australia with him, and the two were married later that year. This major life change was soon followed by another when, in that same year, Singleman met renowned BASE jumper Nic Feteris. Feteris was planning to jump from one of the world's highest cliffs with only a small parachute packed into a backpack in an attempt to break previous world records for height in BASE jumping.

Although Singleman had never jumped from any height with a parachute, he was drawn to the endeavor by his spirit of adventure and his desire to film the expedition. Just as Singleman had no experience jumping, Feteris had never climbed a mountain before. Both men would have to learn new skills in order to successfully complete their goal of BASE jumping from such a high peak. The two over-

Accomplished in both BASE jumping and filmmaking, Singleman prepares to shoot his next feat.

looked their mutual lack of experience and figured that one would make up for the other's deficiencies in either area. They began searching for the most suitable cliff, finding Pakistan's 20,442-foot Great Trango Tower, with its sheer overhanging cliffs and flat landing pad below, to be an optimal choice.

In 1991, BASE jumping was a relatively new sport with few participants worldwide, and Feteris was one of the sport's earliest pioneers. He vowed to teach Singleman, who was always eager to set new goals and challenges for himself, the fundamentals of BASE jumping. The two immediately began training for the Trango Tower jump.

Training for the Ultimate Jump

Singleman first began his training by bungee jumping off of bridges with a mock parachute attached to his back. He then experienced jumping from higher altitudes by skydiving more than fifty times from a plane. Once he got used to falling and deploying his chute, he then did a real BASE jump from a three-hundred-foot crane at the Australian Motorcycle Grand Prix. He describes his first jump:

> About a million things go through your mind in two seconds, but I have to keep control of all of the emotions I have to keep my body upright. I have to be there when the parachute opens so that I can steer it properly. I have to be able to land. All of these things are being eaten away at by this fear and by this adrenaline and by this overwhelming sensation that is entirely new and that's part of the thrill. It's like squeezing your whole life into three seconds.[57]

Singleman jumped three times that day. The first two attempts went well, with the chute deploying and Singleman landing fine. On his third jump, however, the lines in his chute were twisted and he spun out of control, hitting a hot dog stand upon landing. Although he was not seriously injured, the experience shook him up a great deal. There would be no margin for error on the Great Trango Tower, and a miscalculation like this one could have tragic results.

Singleman and Feteris continued to train throughout the end of 1991 and the beginning of 1992, jumping off of the Sydney Harbor Bridge, climbing and canyoning in the nearby Blue Mountains, and putting together the necessary funding for the trip from sponsors and film studios. Although this training gave him confidence, Singleman would face different challenges jumping from a cliff rather than a bridge. If he did not have immediate control of his chute, he stood the chance of smashing into the rock wall on the way down.

Altitude also greatly affects judgment, so he would have to focus all of his attention on performing even the most basic of tasks.

Singleman and Feteris arrived in Pakistan in early summer 1992. They began acclimating themselves to the altitude and made their journey to the Trango Tower. It took them several weeks just to reach their base camp at the cliff's bottom. They were joined by a film crew, porters to carry their supplies, and Singleman's wife, Irina. Although she did not fully support his decision to climb and jump, she felt more comfortable being there than alone at home.

Storming Trango Tower

Although the climb was slow at first, the two men made their way to the summit over the course of several days and scouted out the perfect overhanging ledge to jump from that would afford them the most distance possible from the wall below. While the cameras filmed from below, Singleman huddled next to Feteris on the small ledge more than nineteen thousand feet above sea level, contemplating his next move. Over a year of training had led him to this precipice, and now he had to choose whether to carry out his plans or cling to his fears of "what if." He held tightly to the pilot chute in his hand while adjusting the camera atop his helmet, which would capture the drop firsthand. The two men looked at each other, stared off the cliff at the snow-covered landing pad below, and began their countdown: 3, 2, 1, Go. . . . And then together they hurled their bodies into the void below.

Cameras were fastened to their bodies as well to ensure that every angle of the drop would be filmed. After an eight-second-long free fall of roughly 500 meters, the chutes deployed, and the two jumpers navigated their way to a nearby snowfield at the base of the great wall, where the film crew and Irina eagerly awaited them. The entire event from conception to finish was documented in a film called *BASEClimb,* which won twenty-one international awards for adventure documentaries and was screened in over one hundred eighty countries.

After returning from Pakistan, Singleman began giving motivational speeches to schools and businesses about overcoming fear and setting goals. He explains the concept of fear and his reasons for lecturing:

> Only by overcoming fear can we achieve our full potential as human beings, because fear affects us in more ways than we think. . . . Unless we understand what it means to overcome fear, then we are basically the victims of fear. . . . What I

Singleman BASE jumps from Idaho's Perrine Bridge. When time allows, Singleman gives motivational speeches about overcoming fear and setting goals.

learned out of BASE jumping was that it is possible to overcome the most powerful fear you've got. . . . No other fear in everyday life is as intense as running off a cliff. So then I got this incredible sense of humanity and sense of possibility . . . and I felt obliged to tell everyone about it, and that's why I make films . . . and lecture to schools, community groups, and companies about what it means to really take charge of your life and overcome fear. [58]

Contracting a Serious Illness

Singleman gained much insight from his experiences in Pakistan, but he also contracted a serious illness during his stay there. While he held medical clinics for the porters who carried his and Feteris's

Tombstone Cliff in Utah provides a beautiful setting and a five-hundred-foot vertical drop for BASE jumpers like Singleman.

equipment, he noticed that they all had a cough, which he soon developed as well. Upon his return to Australia, Singleman realized that cough was tuberculosis. The disease compromised his lung capacity and made it even harder for him to breathe at high altitudes on his mountain-climbing expeditions. He began a series of treatments, which had him taking up to seventeen pills a day at one point. Though he recovered, complications from the disease would prove to be a recurring problem throughout Singleman's life and would affect the outcome of future expeditions.

Old and New Relationships

Over the next few years, Singleman continued to BASE-jump, lecturing all the while. He also continued to make films, while still working several days a week as an emergency room doctor. He and his wife, Irina, had two sons during this period as well, David in 1993 and Nathan in 1994. As Singleman began to focus more of his energy on BASE jumping and climbing, the couple began to experience problems that ultimately led to their separation in 1995 and their final divorce in 1996.

Shortly after the two separated, Singleman met Heather Swan, who worked in management at a celebrity speaking bureau. The two met at one of his lectures and began dating shortly thereafter. They were married at the end of 1998. She had two children from a previous marriage as well, a boy named Ty who was then twelve and a girl named Lauren who was eight.

Over the course of the next few years, Singleman continued climbing and BASE jumping and worked on several other films. Swan began working in sports management, working with the Australian Olympic Committee in preparation for the Sydney Games. After several years of marriage, Singleman came up with an idea for the film *BASEClimb 2*. An article posted on ABC.net describes the inspiration:

> Heather has heard him say over 100 times "that anyone who could stand on a chair, jump off, and land upright has the physical ability to BASE jump the highest cliff in the world—the only things holding us back are mental barriers." So when Glenn was told about a cliff higher than the one he jumped it was Heather who said, "Here's a chance to prove your theory—train me and together we'll climb and BASE jump this new cliff and you can make *BASEClimb 2*." [59]

BASEClimb 2 Project

In 1999 the two began training for the project. Their goal was to jump from the 22,467-foot peak Ama Dablam in Nepal. They followed some of the same routines that Singleman originally undertook in preparing for Trango Tower. During one of her bungee jumps, Swan tore a hole in her small intestine, which almost ended the project. But determined to make it work, she continued to train by skydiving, jumping from hot-air balloons, and BASE jumping bridges and cliffs in Idaho, Utah, and Italy.

Later that year, when they began climbing Ama Dablam, they found no suitable launch site safe enough to BASE jump from without significant risk of injury or death. Determined not to accept defeat, the couple returned to Trango Tower, the site of Singleman's first big wall jump. But they chose a launch spot about six hundred feet higher than the previous one. Issues with Singleman's preexisting lung condition made preparing for the jump difficult. As he explains, "It was a lot harder for me on the second expedition to climb to the same altitude. It was very frustrating because I have been there before and found it very straightforward and the second time it was just so much harder for me. . . . Since then I've had a lot of lung training and pretty much got back what I lost." [60]

The weather and snow conditions were terrible on their climb up Trango Tower. When they finally did reach the launch site, on September 10, 2001, an avalanche nearly killed the entire party. They decided to retreat to a lower elevation on the mountain to wait out the adverse snow conditions, but the terrorist events the following day in New York made Pakistan and other countries in the Middle East unsafe for tourists. With an impending invasion by U.S. forces in Afghanistan, Singleman and the group returned to Australia downtrodden but not defeated. He describes his thoughts on their decision not to jump:

> BASE jumping is so dangerous that you do not want to be in a position to say "I told you so" later. It's much better to have judgment and be able to say no. . . . It is as dangerous as you choose to make it. If you look at all BASE-jumping accidents, it is almost 100 percent human error if things go wrong and it is usually judgment. . . . We do things the way we do, and we have not been hurt, and we are proud of that fact. [61]

Singleman still made the film *BASEClimb 2,* and it was an even bigger success than his first BASE climbing film. Even though Glenn Singleman and Heather Swan failed to jump from the higher cliff on Trango Tower, they succeeded in achieving their main goal, which was enabling Swan to overcome her fears and self-limiting beliefs. The entire process of training and attempting such a climb and jump proved Singleman's theory that even ordinary people can achieve the extraordinary if they believe in themselves and strive to break their preconceived notion of their own ability to succeed. The film still conveys how teamwork and confronting one's fears can help a person overcome great obstacles, both personal and physical. The film aired on ABC television in the fall of 2002 and also ran in over one hundred other countries on the National Geographic Channel that same year. Singleman and Swan began to lecture together about their experiences overcoming fear. Swan also wrote a book about the Trango Tower experience called *Defying Gravity, Defying Fear: One Woman's Journey,* which was a finalist in the Banff Mountain Book Festival and sold out its first print run.

Singleman parachutes along a cliff face to conclude a BASE jump. Singleman continues to push BASE-jumping limits and shares those experiences through film and lectures.

Exploring Film at the Bottom and Top of the World

Even with his busy lecture schedule, Singleman still found time to occasionally work in the emergency room, and he even set aside time to work on another film. This project took him some twenty thousand feet under the sea in a specially-designed Russian submersible capable of reaching such amazing ocean depths. Singleman assisted the famed Hollywood director James Cameron, and spent August through October of 2003 exploring and filming underwater volcanoes along the hydrothermal vent in both the Atlantic and Pacific oceans. This footage using 3-D high definition cameras will be edited into an upcoming IMAX documentary. Singleman acted as both camera assistant and doctor for the expedition, and he felt privileged to be able to join the crew and learn from an experienced director.

Singleman's upcoming film project is *BASEClimb 3*, which will take him and Swan back to Pakistan to a formation called the Ogre, located a few miles from the Trango Tower. Even though the Ogre stands 23,770 feet tall, they will not go all the way to the summit, which has been reached by only two climbing parties before. They plan to jump from somewhere above 21,300 feet, thereby breaking Singleman's previous record. This expedition will require greater climbing skills and more planning than their previous one, but the couple is optimistic about the outcome. They plan to train in the United States in both Yosemite National Park and California's High Sierra to get used to technical rock climbing at high altitudes.

Philosophy of Goal Setting

Singleman continues to push his limits as a BASE jumper and climber. He shares his experience and knowledge through film, speech, and life example. He explains his motivation as a jumper and an inspirational speaker:

> What we did wasn't crazy at all. It was about overcoming mental boundaries. It was about overcoming our fears. It was about maturing as people. If we were mad, we'd be dead, because BASE jumping is so dangerous. . . . We had to use our judgment to manage the risk and that's a really exciting thing to do. To dream up something and . . . in the process, overcome all of your own fears, shortcomings, and limitations is so incredibly powerful because you discover your dreams. You discover meaningfulness. [62]

CHAPTER 6

Mike Metzger: The Godfather of Freestyle Motocross

Mike Metzger is an all-around athlete on a motorcycle. He has raced motocross since the age of six, performing at high levels over the course of his racing career. In the mid-1990s, Metzger began participating in a little-known sport called freestyle motocross, which was modeled after early bicycle motocross (BMX), with tricks performed on ramps and natural jumps. As a pioneer in freestyle motocross, Metzger has become known as the Godfather to other participants and fans. Mike Metzger has devoted his life to the sport of motorcycle racing and freestyle motocross, and his many accomplishments speak for themselves.

Growing Up Riding

Mike Metzger was born in Huntington Beach, California, on November 19, 1975. His father, Theodore Fritz Metzger, worked in the construction business, and his mother, Sharon, was a homemaker. Mike began riding motorcycles at an early age. Even while he was still in diapers he rode on the seat of his father's and grandfather's bikes. Both older Metzgers had raced motorcycles in their youth; Mike's father, Ted, stopped racing after he broke his back in an accident. Despite suffering this injury, Ted encouraged his son to pick up the sport at an early age and bought him a Suzuki Jr. 50 when Mike was just three years old.

Riding motorcycles was as ordinary to young Mike as riding bicycles is to most children. He began motorcycle racing at the age of six at the nearby Corona Raceway in Corona, California, and he became quite adept, winning many competitions in his age bracket. Mike exhibited fearlessness from the start. As he explains, "I always had the personality for it. Looking back to when I was a kid, the risk factor never meant much to me. I never thought about what the risk would be if I didn't do something successfully. It was like I'm going for it, no matter what the risks are. I'm just going to try it because I want to do it." [63]

Mike also took advantage of the abundance of trails in the area to ride both his motorcycle and bicycle. He began experimenting with jumping his BMX bike on a homemade ramp in his driveway. He loved bike riding as much as motorcycles, hanging out with the local riders doing freestyle tricks on ramps and riding downhill at great speed. If it had two wheels and could go fast, Mike took an interest in it.

Mike's love of riding provided him with endless hours of entertainment, but it also distracted him from schoolwork at times. One motivating factor that kept Mike doing well in school was the family policy that if he got bad grades, he could not ride his motorcycle. Just the thought of not being able to ride kept Mike engaged in his schoolwork. He excelled in art classes throughout middle school and became interested in tattoos and tattoo artistry.

Freestyle Conception and Development

Throughout his early teens, Mike's main interest still revolved around bikes: racing and jumping motorcycles and performing acrobatic stunts on his bicycle. Soon Mike began attempting on his motorcycle the jumps and tricks he did with his bicycle, and a new sport was born. He says, "Freestyle motocross was something that just happened, copying my friends' BMX tricks on my dirt bike. All the while I was doing that, I continued to race motorcycles. We actually began doing freestyle on our own about 1991, years before it became an organized sport." [64] Mike's early introduction to motorcycles made him an ideal contender to revolutionize the sport of motocross. And his natural ability and poise, mixed with a virtual fearlessness of speed and jumps, would enable him to take the sport to a new level.

Throughout the early 1990s Metzger continued to race standard motocross. In 1991 he won the American Motorcyclist Association (AMA) 80cc fourteen- to fifteen-year-old amateur motocross championship, one of the main competitions. He also continued to experiment with new freestyle moves on his own and with a small group of friends. Freestyle motocross differs from racing in that riders navigate their motorcycles over a series of jumps, performing various tricks while in midair, much like a skateboarder or BMX bike rider does on a half-pipe. The term *freestyle motocross* was coined in the early 1990s by motorcycle magazines to describe the stylish tricks and jumps that a handful of riders were attempting.

Most tricks can trace their roots back to early BMX moves performed throughout the 1980s, when that sport gained its initial popularity. Unlike motorcycle races—also called Supercross—where the

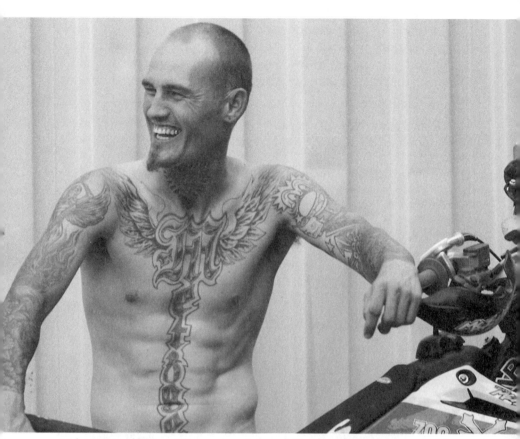

Mike Metzger began riding motorcycles while still wearing diapers, and has since become the world's most recognized freestyle motocross rider.

winner is the person who crosses the finish line first, a freestyle competition is judged on how well a rider performs a series of tricks over a set course in a certain amount of time. At this point in Mike Metzger's career, there were no set competitions and freestyle motocross did not exist in any established form. All of that was about to change, however.

The Birth of a New Sport

When Metzger graduated from high school in 1993, he chose to ride motorcycles instead of going to college. He continued to race motocross but longed for some other means of expression. He also worked as a tattoo artist during this period, actually practicing on himself when there were no customers. He found that self-tattooing does not work very well, because the pain interferes with one's concentration. From then on he let others draw the designs that began to cover his arms and back over the next few years.

In 1996 Metzger's creation of new tricks on his motorcycle earned him the honor of being the first freestyle motocross rider featured on the cover of *Dirt Rider* magazine. Shawn Frederick and Bill Gutman describe some of the moves Metzger performs in their book *Being Extreme:*

> The midair maneuvers can be quite complex, but must be done quickly and with style, since the bike is only high in

Metzger practices a sidewinder air at his backyard track in Southern California. Metzger was one of the first motocross racers to perform freestyle tricks.

the air for a matter of seconds. The names of the tricks are similar to those in skateboarding and BMX freestyle competitions. For example, the *can-can* is accomplished by the rider taking his right or left leg and swinging it over to the opposite side of the bike, in midair, then pointing it outward. Both legs are on the same side of the bike, only one on the peg, or footrest, with the other foot pointing up in the air. . . . The *knack-knack* is done by swinging one leg to the opposite side of the bike with the rider standing with one foot on the peg. [65]

These moves are made even harder when the rider either leaves his feet off of the pegs entirely or chooses to use no hands while executing the maneuver at high speeds in midair.

Freestyle motocross was becoming popular in small circles of riders bored with the routine of racing. Metzger became known as the "Godfather" of freestyle motocross because of his innovative style and seeming fearlessness in attempting these jumps. The sport gained enough popularity that a few years later, in 1998, organized freestyle motocross events began to be held and the new sport was officially recognized by the motocross community. The first freestyle event was held in Las Vegas, Nevada, in May 1998. At that point, Metzger was still racing Supercross, so he was unable to devote all of his time to mastering new freestyle moves. Torn between two sports, and not wanting to compromise his training, Metzger was left wondering which direction to turn.

Switching to Freestyle

An unforeseen event made his decision for him. That spring, Metzger crashed during a race and was trapped between the rear wheel and frame of another racer's bike, receiving a terrible burn on his back. Metzger explains the situation: "I got a third-degree wound across my back, where it tore out some of my lat muscle, and that's pretty much it. . . . It took me six months to heal. Burns aren't fun." [66] Several months later, when Metzger did finally heal, he returned to motocross as a freestyle rider first and foremost and a racer second. Crashes were less likely in freestyle riding and he wanted to explore the seemingly infinite possibilities of this new sport that he had helped to create years earlier.

More freestyle events began to be held nationwide, and more motocross riders became interested in the offshoot of their sport. In 1998 Metzger entered the first-ever Van's Triple Crown Free Air

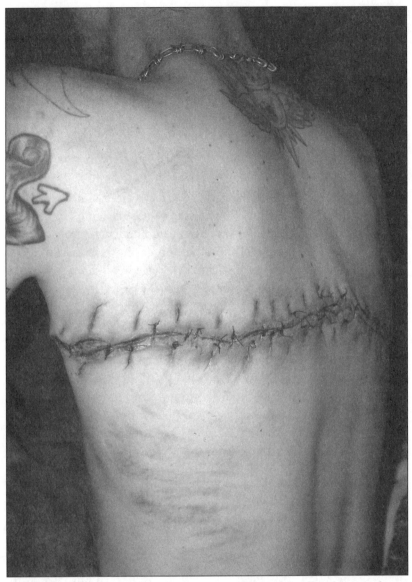

In a 1998 crash during a motocross race, Metzger suffered severe burns and muscle tears to his back. Following the crash, Metzger focused mainly on motocross's freestyle discipline.

Festival, a standard freestyle big-air competition. He won and was crowned the champion for his ability to jump higher than his competitors and perform more outrageous stunts in midair. Freestyle motocross involves a high degree of skill and focus; if a rider fails to negotiate the attempted move, the result could be broken bones, paralysis, or even death. Some stunts that Metzger performed involved both handless and footless landings, and he sometimes fully dismounted the bike in midair, only to grab hold of the bars at the last minute for a smooth landing. This victory gave Metzger a fifty-thousand-dollar prize check and secured his status as the Godfather of freestyle motocross.

Developing a Signature Move

Metzger continued to expand his repertoire of moves and excelled at the sport. In 1999 he returned to the Van's Triple Crown in San Diego and took the contest by storm. He describes his qualifying run, in which a mistake turned into his signature move:

> Back then, the courses were small and in a two-minute run you had to get sixteen tricks off. So I went for the bar hop, which is basically a jump up over the handlebars where you stick your feet out as far as you can, then swing back through the handlebars and land on your pegs. When I went to do the trick, I felt I wouldn't get my legs back over the handlebars, that I would catch the back of my boots on the handlebars and crash. So I just let go of the bars with both hands, swung my legs around the handlebars, grabbed them again, and landed perfectly. [67]

He named this move the McMetz, and it secured his victory at the Triple Crown competition for a second year in a row.

Aside from the Van's Triple Crown, which is held yearly, there are also the Gravity Games and the X Games. Both of these competitions started including freestyle motocross in their lineup. In 2000 Metzger won the silver medal at the Gravity Games, linking his signature move together with a series of other hard tricks.

As freestyle motocross gained notoriety, advertisers took notice and began using the sport to endorse products. In the year 2000, Metzger appeared in a Mountain Dew commercial with fellow freestyle riders Kris Rourke and Travis Pastrana. The commercial aired during that year's Super Bowl, giving maximum exposure to the relatively new sport.

Focusing on Business and Family

Though Metzger still enjoyed freestyle competitions, he considered himself a motorcycle racer at heart. Even after his accident in 1998 and his immense success as a freestyle rider, he missed the speed and focus involved in Supercross and motorcycle racing. However, he looked at freestyle as a way for him to ride full-time. Through sponsorships such as Zoo York, Red Bull, EA Sports, Pro Circuit, VP Racing

Fuels, and prize money, he was able to start his own company, Metzger Motorsports, and focus on riding motorcycles both on the track and over jumps. Run by his mother and his aunt, Cathy Armstrong, the business sells T-shirts, hats, and graphic kits for motorcycles.

Metzger continued to ride in freestyle competitions throughout 2000 and 2001, but he also returned to racing motorcycles as well, riding full-time in both categories. During this period, Metzger also married his girlfriend, Mandi. She supported his desire to race and attended freestyle competitions and races even though it was hard to watch him risk his life at times. The two had a daughter, Michaela Rose, in 2001 and moved to Menifee, California.

Mastering the Backflip

While he was busy with his new family responsibilities and still putting time into racing, Metzger began hatching plans to revolutionize freestyle competition as well. He began practicing backflips on his motorcycle. He explains the process:

> Most people don't want to think about crushing themselves with a 225 pound motorcycle. I had been doing backflips into a foam pit on my BMX bike. I also spent a lot of time on my trampoline thinking about backflips and doing them. Then I took a ramp out to the sand dunes and did two backflips into the dunes. But I didn't have the jump set up at the proper distance, so I had to jump off . . . before I landed. I did that twice and wrecked my bike. A couple weeks later, I got it. [68]

Metzger kept practicing the backflip until he perfected it on his home ramp. His practice paid off when, on July 2, 2002, he became the first freestyle motocross rider to successfully land a backflip over a forty-eight-foot gap on a full-size (225-pound) motorcycle. He accomplished this feat at his backyard Moto-X course, which he designed and used for practice. X Game organizer and president of Moto-X Company Paul Taublieb commented on the miraculous accomplishment:

> Metzger did what was said couldn't be done. A full, floating back flip over a big gap. The sport is constantly progressing and the back flip is almost a metaphor for the sport itself. . . . Fittingly, the man credited with starting the entire freestyle movement, Mike Metzger, busted the door down and sent the sport hurtling into the future. . . . The thing that shocked me the most—and I'm still in a state of shock—

Metzger rotates through a backflip during the first week of practicing the dangerous trick on his home track.

was how graceful and natural Metz made it look. . . . That is what a back flip should look like—the way you would draw it in a notebook.[69]

Metzger performed a total of five backflips that day. Two days later, on Independence Day, he did twenty-one backflips in a row to show his mastery of the trick. He explains the mental and physical process involved in performing this incredible stunt:

> The technique is critical. It looks easy and it looks graceful, but it is not. I put in months of practice. It is all about throttle control off the ramp. When your front tire leaves the ramp, you give it a bit of throttle and don't look back too soon. You can over rotate, so keep steady and the bike will come around by itself. As you get to the top of the jump, the suspension is springing back and you feel that tug, and it helps continue your rotation. You have to learn how to spot the ground, then you do the same types of things that you normally do when landing. I'm so happy. I've been working hard, and I woke up at 5 A.M. today and knew in my heart I was going to try and I was going to do it. The Godfather is back.[70]

The question still remained, however: Could Metzger perform the backflip in competition, on an unfamiliar ramp, with thousands of fans watching? At the Summer X Games in Philadelphia in August 2002, Metzger successfully proved himself in competition when he landed two backflips in a row over an eighty-foot gap. Not only was he the first rider to land a backflip on a full-sized motorcycle, but he had now repeated that feat in front of his fans over a gap almost twice as big as that in his original flips. Metzger raised the level of expectation in freestyle motocross and proved that he was indeed the Godfather of the sport, walking away with the gold.

Pushing the Flip Further

When Metzger arrived at the Winter X Games in Aspen, Colorado, some six months later, he faced some of the toughest competition of his life. Realizing that the backflip had determined the future of the sport, several competitors had practiced and perfected the move. Metzger was one of three freestyle riders (the others were Caleb Wyatt and Nate Adams) to perform a backflip that competition day. Although many opponents thought that he might try the flip on a larger, ninety-foot-jump, Metzger surprised everyone by performing a no-footed backflip, taking his feet off of his pegs while he was upside down and in midflight. Once again, he won the gold medal with a score of 93.3, raising the bar a few notches in the process.

After winning the gold in two X Games in a row and performing revolutionary tricks at both competitions, Metzger wondered what was next for him in the sport of motocross. He had already injured himself severely on numerous occasions and was unsure how much further he could push gravity's limitations. Regarding his past injuries, Metzger says,

> I've probably put myself through hell on earth growing up. Torture I call it. I've broken both my femurs, had rods put in both of them and taken out again. I've had operations on both knees, broke both wrists several times, broke my back three times. I'm already full of arthritis. . . . But I train harder than at any time in my life and I'm ready to take on the world.[71]

In classic Metzger style, he boosts a nac-nac flip during a Winter X Games freestyle run. Several competitors added the backflip into their freestyle runs after Metzger landed the first one in 2002.

Switching Focus

Metzger began to weigh his options once again. He could continue to compete in freestyle competitions, more than likely placing in several more with his signature backflip and variations on it. He could also focus entirely on Supercross racing and continue to ride his motorcycle in that manner. He was torn between which direction to turn.

Metzger leans into a turn during a Supermoto race in 2003. Metzger plans to enter more Supermoto events in the future and fewer freestyle contests.

In the spring of 2003, Mike Metzger announced that he would not compete in the Global X Games, the Summer X Games, the Gravity Games, or any other upcoming freestyle competition. He explained this decision in a press release: "My passion has always been racing. . . . I reached a goal in freestyle. That was to prove that I'm the best and my world record feat of back to back back-flips over 50-feet and 80-feet gaps made that statement, and has not yet been approached by any other rider so I'd like to move on to another challenge that involves racing." [72]

Metzger chose to enter a new form of racing called Supermoto. The sport involves high-speed racing on a larger bike than what Metzger rode freestyle or Supercross, racing over a course of mixed road and trail. He looks forward to the new challenge and hopes to bring innovation to this sport as well. Backed by American Honda Motor Company, Metzger races a CRF450R motorcycle. He says of his early experience with the new sport and the new motorcycle, "It really suits my style on both the dirt and pavement sections of the Supermoto course. I've already won some early season races on it and my confidence grows every time I ride it. I can't wait for the AMA series to start so I can take all the training and riding I've been doing to the racetrack and bring home some results on this bike." [73]

Mike Metzger currently lives in Menifee, California, with his wife, daughter, and son, Myrie, who was born in December 2003. He continues to ride freestyle for personal pleasure and at various demos set up by his many sponsors. He looks forward to pushing his boundaries of freestyle motocross and pursuing his career in Supermoto as a new means of expressing himself through the familiar medium of the motorcycle.

NOTES

Introduction: The Nature of the Extreme Athlete

1. Brendan I. Koerner, "Extreeme," in Dick Wimmer, ed., *The Extreme Game: An Extreme Sports Anthology*. Springfield, NJ: Burford Books, 2001, p. 7.

2. Quoted in Koerner, "Extreeme," p. 3.

3. Quoted in Maryann Karinch, *Lessons from the Edge: Extreme Athletes Show You How to Take on High Risk and Succeed*. New York: Fireside Books, 2000, p. 19.

Chapter 1: Laird Hamilton: The Art of Tow-In Surfing

4. Quoted in Bruce Jenkins, "Laird Hamilton," in John Long, ed., *The Big Drop: Classic Big Wave Surfing Stories*. Guilford, CT: Falcon Press, 1999, p. 196.

5. Quoted in LairdHamilton.com, "Laird Hamilton Biography," www.lairdhamilton.com/bio.htm.

6. Quoted in Bucky McMahon, "The Hydroponic Dreams of Laird Hamilton," June 1994. www.outside.away.com/magazine/0694/946fsurf.html.

7. Quoted in Jenkins, "Laird Hamilton," p. 205.

8. Quoted in McMahon, "The Hydroponic Dreams of Laird Hamilton."

9. Quoted in Matt Warshaw, *Mavericks: The Story of Big Wave Surfing*. San Francisco: Chronicle Books, 2000, p. 157.

10. Joel Achenbach, "In the Teeth of Jaws," *National Geographic,* November 1998, p. 64.

11. Quoted in Warshaw, *Mavericks,* p. 157.

12. Quoted in Warshaw, *Mavericks,* p. 157.

13. Quoted in Ken Bradshaw, "A Farewell to Arms," www.kenbradshaw.com/stories/farewelltoarms.html.

14. Quoted in Jamie Brown, "Surfing the Set from Hell," September 6, 2000. www.weather-wise.com/surf/teahupo-o.htm.

15. Quoted in *Laird,* video, dir. Bluefield Entertainment/Laird Hamilton, 2001.

16. Quoted in *Laird.*

17. Quoted in LairdHamilton.com, "Laird Hamilton Biography."

Chapter 2: Dan Osman: Pushing Gravity's Limits

18. Quoted in Todd Worsfold, "Beyond the Door," *Climbing*, April/May 1993, p. 168.

19. Quoted in Craig Vetter, "Terminal Velocity," *Outside*, April 1999. http://outside.away.com/magazine/0499/9904terminal.html.

20. Quoted in Worsfold, "Beyond the Door," p. 168.

21. Quoted in Vetter, "Terminal Velocity."

22. Quoted in *Outside*, "The Outside Prognosticator: Really Quite Stupid," January 1996. www.outside.away.com/outside/magazine/0196/janfea.html.

23. Quoted in Eric Perlman, "The Life and Death of Dan Osman," *Rock and Ice Magazine*, February 1999, no. 90, p. 86.

24. Quoted in Vetter, "Terminal Velocity."

25. Quoted in Vetter, "Terminal Velocity."

Chapter 3: Kristen Ulmer: Freeskiing Pioneer

26. Quoted in Shawn Frederick and Bill Gutman, *Being Extreme*. New York: Citadel Press, 2002, p. 26.

27. Kristen Ulmer, phone interview with author, November 16, 2003.

28. Ulmer, phone interview with author.

29. Ulmer, phone interview with author.

30. Quoted in Frederick and Gutman, *Being Extreme*, pp. 130–31.

31. Ulmer, phone interview with author.

32. Quoted in Frederick and Gutman, *Being Extreme*, pp. 33–34.

33. Quoted in Frederick and Gutman, *Being Extreme*, p. 132.

34. Quoted in Frederick and Gutman, *Being Extreme*, p. 133.

35. Kristen Ulmer, "Cliffhanger," *Skiing*, February 2001, p. 111.

36. Quoted in Ben Tiffany, "Ulmer's." www.skiersjournal.com/article.php?sid=782.

37. Quoted in Gary Hook, "The Original Goddess of Extreme," January 12, 2001. www.active.com/story.cfm?story_id=6085.

Chapter 4: Tao Berman: The Art of Extreme Paddling

38. Tao Berman, phone interview with author, November 23, 2003.

39. Berman, phone interview with author.

40. Quoted in Lars Larsson, "Tao Berman Interview," www.freestyle kayaker.com/interviews/tao/tao.html.

41. Berman, phone interview with author.

42. Christian Knight, "In the Cauldron Below," www.taoberman.com/stories.htm#story1.

43. Knight, "In the Cauldron Below."

44. Berman, phone interview with author.

45. Berman, phone interview with author.

46. Quoted in Kelly King, Lars Anderson, and Troy Patterson, "Kayaking: Tao Berman: Legend of the Fall," *Sports Illustrated,* May 28, 2001, p. A31.

47. Knight, "In the Cauldron Below."

48. Quoted in Larsson, "Tao Berman Interview."

49. Berman, phone interview with author.

50. Berman, phone interview with author.

51. Quoted in Rippin Productions, "Tao Berman: Professional Kayaker." www.rippinproductions.com/bio.html.

52. Berman, phone interview with author.

53. Quoted in King, Anderson, and Patterson, "Kayaking: Tao Berman," p. A31.

Chapter 5: Glenn Singleman: BASE-Jumping Visionary

54. Glenn Singleman, phone interview with author, November 28, 2003.

55. Singleman, phone interview with author.

56. Singleman, phone interview with author.

57. Quoted in *BASEClimb,* video, dir. Glenn Singleman, 1993.

58. Singleman, phone interview with author.

59. Quoted in TV Documentaries: Australian Broadcasting Corporation, *BASEClimb 2: Defying Gravity,* www.abc.net.au/documentaries/programs/2000/baseclimb2.htm.

60. Singleman, phone interview with author.

61. Singleman, phone interview with author.

62. Singleman, phone interview with author.

Chapter 6: Mike Metzger: The Godfather of Freestyle Motocross

63. Quoted in Frederick and Gutman, *Being Extreme,* p. 30.

64. Quoted in Frederick and Gutman, *Being Extreme,* p. 157.

65. Frederick and Gutman, *Being Extreme,* pp. 157–58.

66. Quoted in Dino Scoppettone, "Flippin' over the Godfather," www.ea sportsbig.com/articles/metzint.jsp.

67. Quoted in Frederick and Gutman, *Being Extreme,* pp. 159–60.

68. Quoted in Matt Higgins, "Mike Metzger Flipping Out," *Sports Illustrated for Kids,* November 1, 2002, p. 58.

69. Quoted in Alex Thompson, "Metzger Throws It Down," July 3, 2002. www.expn.go.com/mtx/freeridemotox/s/020703_metz flip.html.

70. Quoted in Thompson, "Metzger Throws It Down."

71. Quoted in Frederick and Gutman, *Being Extreme,* p. 199.

72. Quoted in Paul Carruthers, "Freestyle—No More Freestyle for Metzger!" April 21, 2003. www.cyclenews.com/ShowStory.asp? HeadlineID=4635.

73. Quoted in AMA Pro Racing, "Honda Teams Up with Metzger to Bring Performance First to Supermoto," June 5, 2003. www.ama proracing.com/features/03/metzgersupermoto.asp.

Books

Scott Bass, *Surf!: Your Guide to Longboarding, Shortboarding, Tubing, Aerials, Hanging Ten, and More.* Washington, DC: National Geographic Society, 2003. This small book explains the basics of surfing with a brief synopsis of surf culture.

Peter Dixon, *The Complete Guide to Surfing.* Guilford, CT: Lyons Press, 2001. Describes the history and basics of surfing, with information about Laird Hamilton and the evolution of big-wave surfing.

Sam George, ed., *The Perfect Day: 40 Years of* Surfer *Magazine.* San Francisco: Chronicle Books, 2001. Great collage of pictures and information from *Surfer* magazine, with basic information on Laird Hamilton and the evolution of tow-in surfing.

David Gonzales, *Jackson Hole on a Grand Scale.* Boulder, CO: Mountain Sports Press, 2001. Describes the Grand Teton descent and explains freeskiing in the Jackson Hole area.

Eric Jackson, *Whitewater Paddling Strokes and Concepts.* Mechanicsburg, PA: Stackpole Books, 1999. Top paddler Eric Jackson gives advice on kayaking for beginners and intermediates.

Drew Kampion, *Stoked: A History of Surf Culture.* Los Angeles: General, 1997. This book gives a detailed history of surfing and surf culture.

Bruce Lessels, *AMC Whitewater Handbook.* Boston: Appalachian Mountain Club Books, 1994. A basic handbook for white-water kayaking providing techniques and introductory information.

John Long, *How to Rock Climb.* Guilford, CT: Falcon Press, 2004. This book explains the basics of rock climbing and describes the skills necessary to reach an intermediate level at the sport.

Charles Lyon, *Jaws Maui.* Hong Kong: Everbest, 1997. This book has vivid pictures and a wonderful description of the Jaws surf break at Peahi.

Warren Miller, *Warren Miller's Ski Fever.* Del Mar, CA: Tehabi Books, 1995. Great photo exposé of extreme skiing by filmmaker Warren Miller; also explains different ski genres, including freeskiing.

Robert E. Rinehart and Cynthia Sydnor, eds., *To the Extreme: Alternative Sports Inside and Out.* Albany: State University of New York Press, 2003. Describes a multitude of extreme sports, including big-wave surfing, kayaking, and skiing.

Pat Ryan, *World of Sports: Rock Climbing*. Mankato, MN: Smart Apple Media, 2000. A book on the basic history of rock climbing, including brief information on Dan Osman and his climbs and falls.

Pete Takeda, *Climb!: Your Guide to Bouldering, Sport Climbing, Trad Climbing, Ice Climbing, Alpinism, and More*. Washington, DC: National Geographic Society, 2002. This book explains the basics of rock climbing with a focus on both sport climbing and big-wall climbing.

Andrew Todhunter, *Fall of the Phantom Lord*. New York: Anchor Books, 1998. Describes Dan Osman's life and his rise to fame as a rock climber and free-faller.

Videos

BASEClimb 2. Dir. Glenn Singleman. 2002.

Masters of Stone 5. Dir. Eric Perlman. 2000.

Pure Force: Masters of Stone 4. Dir. Eric Perlman. 1998.

Twitch. Dir. Eric Link. 1999.

Twitch 2000. Dir. Eric Link. 2000.

Web Sites

Glenn Singleman Official Web site (www.baseclimb.com). Contains stories and links to biographical information for both Glenn Singleman and Heather Swan. It also contains information on their public speaking business, product information on videos and books, and contact information.

Kristen Ulmer Official Web site (www.xmission.com/~ulmer). Kristen Ulmer's Web site contains biographical information, samples of her articles (both published and unpublished), sponsor links, photos, Ski to Live seminar information, and contact information.

Laird Hamilton Official Web site (www.lairdhamilton.com). Laird Hamilton's Web site includes a biography, career highlights, sponsor links, stories, and pictures.

Mike Metzger Official Web site (www.mikemetzger.com). Mike Metzger's home page contains mostly product information and sponsor links, as well as contact information.

Tao Berman Official Web site (www.taoberman.com). Kayaker Tao Berman's home page includes a biography, paddling stories, descriptions of his world-record descents, contact information, and pictures.

Works Consulted

Books

Shawn Frederick and Bill Gutman, *Being Extreme*. New York: Citadel Press, 2002. An overview of extreme sports with in-depth explanations of motocross, rope jumping, and extreme skiing as well as a variety of other dangerous endeavors. Included in the book are detailed stories about Kristen Ulmer, Mike Metzger, and Dan Osman.

Maryann Karinch, *Lessons from the Edge: Extreme Athletes Show You How to Take on High Risk and Succeed*. New York: Fireside Books, 2000. This book discusses a multitude of extreme sports including BASE jumping, surfing, freeskiing, kayaking, and climbing. It provides insight into not only how the sports are done but also why people choose to risk their lives in the pursuit of the extreme.

John Long, ed., *The Big Drop: Classic Big Wave Surfing Stories*. Guilford, CT: Falcon Press, 1999. A compilation of thirty-two stories about the evolution of big-wave surfing, beginning in the 1950s and ending in the present day. The book contains an abundance of information about Laird Hamilton and his contributions to surfing big waves.

Matt Warshaw, *Mavericks: The Story of Big Wave Surfing*. San Francisco: Chronicle Books, 2000. This book contains detailed information about the evolution of big-wave surfing as well as Laird Hamilton's role in pioneering the sport.

Dick Wimmer, ed., *The Extreme Game: An Extreme Sports Anthology*. Springfield, NJ: Burford Books, 2001. A collection of previously published articles and stories about extreme sports. Included in it are articles about BASE jumping, climbing, kayaking, and freeskiing.

Periodicals

Joel Achenbach, "In the Teeth of Jaws," *National Geographic*, November 1998.

Matt Higgins, "Mike Metzger Flipping Out," *Sports Illustrated for Kids*, November 1, 2002.

Kelly King, Lars Anderson, and Troy Patterson, "Kayaking: Tao Berman: Legend of the Fall," *Sports Illustrated*, May 28, 2001.

Eric Perlman, "The Life and Death of Dan Osman," *Rock and Ice Magazine*, February 1999, no. 90.

Kristen Ulmer, "Cliffhanger," *Skiing*, February 2001.

Todd Worsfold, "Beyond the Door," *Climbing*, April/May 1993.

Internet Sources

AMA Pro Racing, "Honda Teams Up with Metzger to Bring Performance First to Supermoto," June 5, 2003. www.amaproracing.com/features/03/metzgersupermoto.asp.

Ken Bradshaw, "A Farewell to Arms," www.kenbradshaw.com/stories/farewelltoarms.html.

Jamie Brown, "Surfing the Set from Hell," September 6, 2000. www.weather-wise.com/surf/teahupo-o.htm.

Paul Carruthers, "Freestyle—No More Freestyle for Metzger!" April 21, 2003. www.cyclenews.com/ShowStory.asp?HeadlineID=4635.

Gary Hook, "The Original Goddess of Extreme," January 12, 2001. www.active.com/story.cfm?story_id=6085.

Christian Knight, "In the Cauldron Below," www.taoberman.com/stories.htm#story1.

LairdHamilton.com, "Laird Hamilton Biography," www.lairdhamilton.com/bio.htm.

Lars Larsson, "Tao Berman Interview," www.freestylekayaker.com/interviews/tao/tao.html.

Bucky McMahon, "The Hydrophonic Dreams of Laird Hamilton," June 1994. www.outside.away.com/magazine/0694/946fsurf.html.

Outside, "The Outside Prognosticator: Really Quite Stupid," January 1996. www.outside.away.com/outside/magazine/0196/janfea.html.

Rippin Productions, "Tao Berman: Professional Kayaker," www.rippinproductions.com/bio.html.

Dino Scoppettone, "Flippin' over the Godfather," www.easportsbig.com/articles/metzint.jsp.

Alex Thompson, "Metzger Throws It Down," July 3, 2002. www.expn.go.com/mtx/freeridemotox/s/020703_metzflip.html.

Ben Tiffany, "Ulmer's." www.skiersjournal.com/article.php?sid=782.

TV Documentaries: Australian Broadcasting Corporation, *BASEClimb 2: Defying Gravity,* www.abc.net.au/documentaries/programs/2000/baseclimb2.htm.

Craig Vetter, "Terminal Velocity," *Outside,* April 1999. http://outside.away.com/magazine/0499/9904terminal.html.

Videos

BASEClimb. Dir. Glenn Singleman. 1993.

Laird. Dir. Bluefield Entertainment/Laird Hamilton. 2001.

INDEX

PICTURE CREDITS

ABOUT THE AUTHOR

Ron Horton is an English teacher and freelance writer who lives in Portland, Oregon. Originally from the Southeast, he grew up exploring the Blue Ridge Mountains of Virginia and North Carolina. In his spare time, he enjoys rock climbing, snowboarding, and fly-fishing with his black Labrador, Cody.